MW01293679

Self-Denial

Self-Denial

A New Testament View

STUART T. ROCHESTER

CASCADE *Books* · Eugene, Oregon

SELF-DENIAL
A New Testament View

Copyright © 2019 Stuart T. Rochester. All rights reserved. Except for brief quotations in critical publications or reviews, no part of this book may be reproduced in any manner without prior written permission from the publisher. Write: Permissions, Wipf and Stock Publishers, 199 W. 8th Ave., Suite 3, Eugene, OR 97401.

Cascade Books
An Imprint of Wipf and Stock Publishers
199 W. 8th Ave., Suite 3
Eugene, OR 97401

www.wipfandstock.com

PAPERBACK ISBN: 978-1-5326-0382-2
HARDCOVER ISBN: 978-1-5326-0384-6
EBOOK ISBN: 978-1-5326-0383-9

Cataloguing-in-Publication data:

Names: Rochester, Stuart T., author.

Title: Self-denial : a New Testament view. / Stuart T. Rochester.

Description: Eugene, OR: Cascade Books, 2019. | Includes bibliographical references and index.

Identifiers: ISBN 978-1-5326-0382-2 (paperback) | ISBN 978-1-5326-0384-6 (hardcover) | ISBN 978-1-5326-0383-9 (ebook)

Subjects: LCSH: Self-denial. | Suffering—Religious aspects—Christianity—History of doctrines. | Suffering—Biblical teaching. | Bible. New Testament—Criticism, interpretation, etc.

Classification: BS2545.S9 R6 2019 (paperback) | BS2545.S9 (ebook)

Manufactured in the U.S.A.   10/09/19

Scripture quotations, unless otherwise noted, are from New Revised Standard Version Bible, copyright © 1989 National Council of the Churches of Christ in the United States of America. Used by permission. All rights reserved worldwide.

Contents

Introduction

Readers of the Gospels are confronted with a "hard saying" of Jesus: "If any want to become my followers, let them deny themselves and take up their cross and follow me" (Mark 8:34 NRSV). These words echo throughout the New Testament, insisting that self-denial is a requirement for faithful followers of Jesus.

Talk of self-denial would seem to run counter to the idolatry of the self that is evident in much of our increasingly narcissistic contemporary "selfie" culture.[1] There is no doubt that today our society is in the grip of a burgeoning radical individualism—the belief system in which the self is central. While it is unquestionably true that we have a right to think for ourselves, and to make our own decisions about how to live life, there seems to be a pervasive preoccupation, indeed obsession, with defining our own personal identity. In this scenario, any talk of "denying oneself" is going to be unpopular. It seems unnatural. It challenges our innate human tendency to self-centeredness, and goes against all our instincts for self-preservation.

Part of the reason for this unpopularity is that there has been a radical shift in the values of our dominant culture, which has become overwhelmingly secular. Our society generally attempts to conduct itself as if God doesn't exist.[2] This book, however, aims to take seriously what the New Testament says about our human nature and about the principles of human conduct that honor God as the giver of life. It demonstrates that the New Testament writers advocated an attitude of self-denial that issues from the teachings and example of Jesus. When this attitude is translated into committed action, it proves to be life-giving and community-building. Responsible interpretation of the New Testament texts also enables readers

1. See, e.g., Manne, *Life of I.* See also earlier treatments of the subject by Lasch, *Culture of Narcissism*; and Lasch, *Minimal Self.*

2. See, e.g., Gay, *Way of the (Modern) World.*

to distinguish between legitimate self-denial and some questionable ascetic practices such as those flavored with self-neglect, self-negation, and self-affliction.

On the other hand, it needs to be said that a biblical perspective on self-denial is in no way inimical to a biblical perspective on self-love. Jesus' command to "love your neighbor as (you love) yourself" implies his recognition that most of us actually practice *agapē* in regard to ourselves. That is, we feed ourselves, protect ourselves, and seek what we think is good for us. For followers of Christ, an authentic love of self is founded on a deep conviction that we are created, owned, gifted, and honored children of God. These things are not to be denied.

My attempt to speak meaningfully about self-denial raises a set of large and complex philosophical and psychological questions about the nature of the "self" and the formation of identity.[3] Although these questions are beyond the scope of this book, I believe that what Jesus meant by "denying oneself" is discoverable and indeed applicable to us in our time. However, it is essential to recognize that the social milieu in which Jesus operated, and in which the New Testament was written, was different in many ways from that of today. Consciousness of one's place and identity as a member of a group (a family, guild, or religious faction) was critical. Consequently, the meaning of "self" in the first century (and therefore the meaning of "self-denial") was rooted, not in a psychology of individuality, but in a social system that placed a high value on communality. These social foundations relied to a large extent on an honor/shame value system. Honor is the public affirmation of worth, either ascribed or acquired, and shame is a public denial of worth, i.e., dishonor or disgrace. Jesus lived in a mix of cultures in which honor and shame were controlling values. Therefore, an examination of Jesus' words in the Gospels needs to recognize these concepts.[4]

Some readers may wonder (or object) that I have drawn attention to some passages that do not speak directly of self-denial. Much of the New Testament deals not with "denying oneself" as such (only Jesus uses this expression in the Gospels) but with denying sinful attitudes and actions, and giving attention to self-discipline and self-control. My reason for examining this material lies in the importance of the theological anthropology of

3. See, e.g., Taylor's important historical analysis, *Sources of the Self.*

4. These concepts have been well documented. See, e.g., Neufeld and DeMaris, *Understanding the Social World;* or Neyrey and Stewart, *Social World of the New Testament.* For a brief review, see my previous work, "Honor as a Foundation."

the New Testament. Mark 7:21–23 comes close to being a formal statement of an anthropological principle: "It is from within, from the human heart, that evil intentions come" (7:21). The implication is that we human persons are, at our center, fundamentally distorted. Jesus invites us to follow him because he is leading us out of the mess we are in.

Paul's anthropology substantiates this perspective. In short, "All have sinned and fall short of the glory of God" (Rom 3:23). Thus, to understand and practice self-denial we need to come to terms with the fallenness of the deepest levels of our human nature—our minds and hearts. When we recognize that sinful attitudes are embedded in us so that they have become integral parts of our "self" it is possible to "deny" those parts—not to deny their existence, but to say *no* to their power over us, to refuse to let them control us, to reject their insistence that we express them or act them out. To this extent we "deny ourselves." This is only one aspect of self-denial, but it is an important one, and therefore we will give attention to self-control and self-discipline in what follows.

Chapters 1 and 2 will deal in detail with the foundational texts about self-denial and their interpretation in the Gospels. Readers may notice that these two chapters have a more academic tone. This is because I have included in this book, in a modified form, much of the material from my previous unpublished work on self-denial in the Synoptic Gospels. In these chapters I have taken an approach that owes much to the insights of social-scientific criticism. While I believe that this is a valid and fruitful approach, other approaches might well add value.

Chapters 3 and 4 will examine the letters of the earliest Christians— Paul, Peter, James, John, and other anonymous writers—to see how they support Jesus' self-denial sayings by supplying more explicit motivations, some specific examples, and some implications for practical application. This material is, of course, much more diverse, and any analysis of its complexities must concede that there is more than one way of looking at it. Since there is a lot of biblical material to be covered, it is necessary to be quite selective, so in these two chapters the exegesis is not so detailed. The letters are treated in the order in which they appear in the English Bible.

I suggest that this book should be read alongside an open Bible. There are many references to biblical passages, and there is not enough space in this book to quote them all. Please find and read the texts yourself in order to check the validity of my exegesis and reflections.

Although this book concentrates on the New Testament, I recognize that the foundations of self-denial (properly understood) lie deeply within the Scriptures of Israel. The Torah, the Prophets, and the Writings insist that a life characterized by *shalom* must be oriented toward God, not oneself.

Since this book is essentially an academic and exegetical study, practical and pastoral applications of the biblical self-denial concept in contemporary Christian life have not been discussed. I have accumulated a wealth of material for reflection on the ways in which self-denial can be appropriately expressed in individual and communal ways, but this will await the writing of another book.

I wish to thank especially Dr. Sven Soderlund, who supervised some of my research on this topic at Regent College, Vancouver, as well as my colleagues Dr. Derek Tidball, Dr. John Nolland, Dr. Stephen C. Barton, and my wife, Dr. Kathleen Rochester, who all gave helpful comments on drafts of this book. Thanks are also due to the principal, staff, and readers of Tyndale House, Cambridge, where additional research and writing was done. I also thank Mrs. Martry Cole and the leaders of Hope Christian Centre Hobart for allowing me to use her wonderful artwork on the cover.

CHAPTER 1

Jesus' Self-Denial Sayings

THE SELF-DENIAL SAYINGS IN MARK'S GOSPEL
(MARK 8:34–38)

Self-denial is one of the topics about which Christians might wish that Jesus had been more explicit, since it has prompted a variety of interpretations. Although much of the Gospel material is relevant to the topic, only once in Jesus' recorded teachings do the words "let him deny himself" (*aparnēsasthō heauton*) occur.

> If any wish to follow after me, let them deny themselves, and take up their cross and follow me. For those who want to save their life will lose it, but those who lose their life for my sake and the gospel's will save it. (Mark 8:34–35)[1]

These two verses are found also in the Gospels of Matthew and Luke, who almost certainly wrote their versions later. This challenging (even shocking) passage mentions self-denial without explicit clarification, in association with mysterious figurative language about "taking up the cross," and a paradoxical saying about saving and losing lives. These "self-denial" sayings present a challenge for exegesis, since their meaning is not immediately clear. In seeking an authentic reconstruction of what these words would

---

1. I have chosen to make my English translations gender-inclusive by using plural forms instead of the masculine singular. The translations generally follow the NRSV.

have meant to first-century Christians, questions such as these must be asked:

- What does "self-denial" entail?
- What concept of "self" does "self-denial" require?
- How is "self-denial" related to "taking up the cross" and "following" Jesus?
- How is it related to "losing one's life" and "saving" it, and what do these expressions mean?
- What would be the motivation for a person to self-deny?
- How would "self-denial" be related to the social, cultural, and spiritual sensitivities of the original disciples?
- Do Jesus or the Gospel writers elsewhere clarify the meaning of these sayings?

Of course, Jesus' audiences may have had no need to ask these questions, at least not in this modern form. While seeking answers to these exegetical problems, however, Christians in our time will do well to give attention also to the hermeneutical problem: what does self-denial mean for us? The difficulties involved in interpreting these sayings for Christians today stem from several sources.

First, we have inherited two thousand years of Christian history in which these sayings have already been interpreted in diverse ways. Influential writings and practices of our Christian forebears have shaped our concepts of self-denial in ways which may or may not truly reflect the original intention of the sayings.

Second, the great social and intellectual changes brought about over the last 200 to 300 years of secularization, industrialization, and education have resulted in a cultural gap that has distanced us from the milieu of the biblical societies and their ways of thinking and behaving. Not only do we participate in a vastly different kind of society in which we employ a much greater degree of personal autonomy (at least in the West) but we have also become accustomed to thinking of "self" in highly individualized terms, often using well-developed psychological language. We relate to ourselves and to others in patterns different from those of the first century.

The problem of self-denial, then, is twofold. We must first understand it, as best we can, from the perspective of the New Testament writers. We must then recontextualize it, so that we can receive Jesus' words in ways that not only retain authentic interpretation but also enable their application in our modern cultures, which are often hostile to the idea of self-denial.

> And calling the crowd with his disciples, he said to them,
>
>> A If any want to follow me,
>>
>>> B let them deny themselves
>>>
>>> B' and take up their cross
>>
>> A' and follow me. (Mark 8:34)

Grammatically, this first part of Jesus' saying (I will refer to it as the "following" saying) is in the form of a protasis (A) and a compound apodosis of three parts (B, B' and A'). On the literary level, however, the saying is chiastic: forms of the verb "follow" (*akoloutheō* in A and A') frame two expressions (self-denial and cross-bearing, in B and B' respectively) that appear to be parallel. This parallelism may help to interpret both expressions.[2]

"Following" is used both literally and figuratively in the New Testament. Multitudes literally follow Jesus on his travels without becoming truly committed to his cause (e.g., Matt 4:25; 8:1; 12:15; 14:13). The literal use of the word can be seen even in Matt 19:27–28, where both Peter and Jesus are referring primarily to the Twelve. The figurative use is found in Rev 14:4, where redeemed believers "follow the Lamb wherever he goes." Here in Mark 8:34 and the subsequent verses, Jesus is ostensibly speaking to those physically present who may want to follow him literally, and yet, because he is addressing an apparently general audience ("anyone" and "whoever") and because his words have proved to be universally applicable, it is right to acknowledge a figurative "following." Thus, the possibility of following Jesus is open, even in our own time, to all who desire to enter committed discipleship.[3]

According to this saying, the first requirement is self-denial. The basic meaning of the verb *aparneomai* (and its simpler form *arneomai*) is to "say no" or to "deny" either by giving a negative verbal answer to a question (e.g., Luke 8:45) or by an act of refusal (e.g., Heb 11:24, referring to Moses' refusal

---

2. Malina ("Let Him Deny Himself," 107) utilizes this apparent parallelism as an important element of his social psychological model of self-denial.

3. Hengel (*Charismatic Leader,* 61–63) correctly notes that Jesus' call to "follow" was not directed to *all* who heard him, and that "following Jesus concretely as his disciple, and the related abandonment of family and possessions, cannot have been the condition of participation in the kingdom of God for all."

of Egyptian honors) or of renunciation (e.g., Isa 31:7 LXX, with idols as the object). These instances reflect the classical usage. However, the New Testament and later Christian writings extend the meaning of this verb by using it with reference to denying a *person*, that is, Christ. For example, in Mark 14:30 and 72 Peter denies Jesus; in Acts 3:13, 14 the people of Jerusalem deny/reject Jesus. Only in Mark 8:34 and parallels and in 2 Tim 2:12, 13 is the object of the verb "oneself."[4] This usage naturally leads to the question, what does it mean to deny oneself?

Jesus had just been teaching his disciples that he would undergo great suffering and be rejected (*apodokimazō*) by the elders, the chief priests, and the scribes (Mark 8:31). This rejection could well be what Jesus has in mind when later in the Gospel he refers to himself cryptically as "the stone which the builders rejected (*apodokimazō*)" (Mark 12:10, quoting Ps 118:22). The rejection of Jesus by Israel is expressed as denial/disowning in Acts 3:13, 14: "Jesus, whom you handed over and rejected (*arneomai*) . . . but you rejected (*arneomai*) the Holy and Righteous One." Clearly, the concepts of rejection and denial are very closely related. In an effort to prepare the disciples for rejection similar to his own, Jesus seems to be urging them to be intentional before the time, to deny *themselves* (that is, to reject something about themselves) and to "take up their cross."

The cross was the upright stake on which Romans and others executed their most despised victims; it was the ultimate symbol of shame. To be hung or nailed on a cross was to be subjected to the very depths of dishonor. But it was also, according to the Scriptures, equivalent to being cursed by God (Deut 21:23; Gal 3:13). It's possible that Jesus witnessed criminals carrying their own crossbeams to execution in Galilee during his childhood,[5] and by mentioning it here Jesus is indirectly predicting the means of his own death.[6]

4. See Schlier, "*Arneomai*"; Koch, "Self-Denial."

5. Fletcher, "Condemned to Die," 162. Albright (*Matthew*, 132) says that "long before the time of Jesus, impaling or crucifixion had become typical of violent death" (Plato *Republic* ii. 361; Artemidorus, ii. 56; *Bereshith Rabba* on Gen 22:6). See also Griffiths, "Disciple's Cross," 358–64.

6. Seccombe, "Take Up Your Cross," 141. Some scholars (e.g., Wrede and Bultmann) have assumed that this prediction is a secondary construction of the church, but the Gospels show that Jesus' life was increasingly in danger, and it is likely that, because of the Sanhedrin's unwillingness to conduct an execution themselves, for reasons of both legality and prudence, a Roman crucifixion would be the only and inevitable option (Seccombe, "Take Up Your Cross," 142–44). In addition, Jesus may have desired that his disciples, in conformity to their teacher, should share this death with him, carrying their

A For those who want to save their life

> B will lose it,

> B' and those who lose their life for my sake, and for the sake of the gospel,

A' will save it. (Mark 8:35)

This saying, which I will refer to as the "saving/losing" saying, is chiastic like the previous one, and stands as a reason for and explanation of the previous saying about following, self-denial, and cross-bearing. It underlines the life-and-death dimension of these activities. The possibility of death for disciples is made explicit here, but along with it there is salvation. The saying is paradoxical, but its meaning is fairly clear: the active pursuit of preservation of life will result in a loss which is equivalent to destruction, but the active pursuit of discipleship, with the risk of losing one's life, will result in salvation.

The words "for my sake" (literally "on account of me") are important, as they indicate the christological focus of self-denying behavior, setting it apart from secular forms of self-renunciation and altruism. The phrase appears in various forms in the Synoptic Gospels: on account of Jesus and his name, his followers will leave homes and families (Mark 10:29 and parallels), be persecuted (Matt 5:11), be hated by all (Mark 13:13 and parallels), and be delivered up to hostile authorities (Mark 13:9 and parallels). These passages seem to echo Ps 44:22, "For your sake we are being killed all day long," which Paul quotes in Rom 8:36. In other words, a willingness to lose one's life, to bear the cross of Christ, is contingent on a fundamental loyalty to him. Jesus, and all that he represents (the gospel and the kingdom of God) is held in such honor that all else, including suffering and the possibility of death, is of lesser importance. This attitude is exemplified by the apostle Thomas, who, in John 11:16, says, "Let us go, that we may die with him."

Jesus continues to explain in the next three verses what it means to preserve or lose one's life. The sayings are linked by the repeated use of "for" (Greek *gar*).

> For what will it profit them to gain the whole world and forfeit their life?

> For what can they give in return for their life? (Mark 8:36–37)

---

own crosses to martyrdom (146).

The concepts are presented in economic terms, as two rhetorical questions. The implication of the saying is that there is no ultimate benefit in "gaining the whole world" if it means "forfeiting one's life." To "gain the whole world" may convey the accumulation of material possessions, for the language of gain and loss was often used in commercial transactions. Self-interest, self-aggrandizement, and the pursuit of wealth and honor are activities of those who have lost sight of the reality of salvation. Such unprofitable gain will turn out to be shame, as the next saying explains.

> For those who are ashamed of me and my words in this adulterous and sinful generation, of them the Son of Man will also be ashamed when he comes in the glory of the Father with the holy angels. (Mark 8:38)

This saying explains the basis of the ultimate loss of life that will be suffered by those who are unwilling to deny themselves. There will be eschatological judgment, expressed here in terms of shame. That is, those who will not honor Jesus will not be honored by the Son of Man when he comes in his full glory. The saying thus functions as a strong motivation for the radical discipleship outlined in 8:34. The future coming of Christ, then, will be a scene of shame for some, and (implicitly) an occasion of honor for others. What will determine the outcome is the degree to which disciples honor Jesus in the present time. The saying of Mark 8:38 brings to an eschatological climax the challenging conditions for discipleship presented in this group of sayings. The challenge is one the disciples are in fact not able to meet on the night of Jesus' betrayal. Peter is singled out as the one who verbally denies Jesus before others: "I do not know this man" (Mark 14:66–72).

The Literary Setting (Mark 8:27—9:8) as Honor Discourse

The "self-denial" sayings of Mark 8:34–35, with their subsequent explanatory sayings, are placed appropriately between two related passages. The first presents Peter's confession of Jesus as the Christ, followed by Jesus' passion prediction (Mark 8:27–33). The second narrates the transfiguration of Jesus (Mark 9:2–8). This pattern is the same in all three Synoptic Gospels: Matt 16:13—17:8 and Luke 9:18–36 are the parallels. This larger literary setting contains two great christological statements, that of Peter (8:29) and that of the voice from heaven (9:7), which ground discipleship in the person, purpose, and mission of Jesus. These two passages function as components of an honor discourse.

Peter Honors Jesus

Jesus the teacher asks his disciples, "Who do people say that I am? Who do you say that I am?" (8:27, 29). Jesus hardly needs affirmation of his identity. He is, nevertheless, concerned about his reputation. The question of whose opinion about Jesus carries the most weight will be a crucial one for a prospective disciple. The answers to Jesus' questions indicate that he is already likened to the greatest and most honorable prophets of Israel, e.g., Elijah (v. 28). His rhetorical strategy (or Mark's) may well be to draw out a more appropriate and more specific answer from the estimation of his own disciples.

Peter identifies Jesus as the Christ (Mark 8:29), the honorific title of the long-awaited Messiah of Jewish hopes. However, Jesus warns the disciples to tell no one (8:30). He contradicts the expectation that an honored person is to be publicly acknowledged and praised. The Jewish hopes do not portray a Messiah who suffers and is killed, but rather a conquering national hero who will deliver Israel and usher in the new age on earth. Jesus therefore corrects this idea. He predicts dishonor (suffering, rejection, and murder) at the hands of the traditional "court of reputation" (the elders, chief priests, and scribes).[7] With this revelation (8:31), Jesus points out to his disciples and potential disciples the nature of his journey. Those who hear the self-denial saying, then, already know where Jesus is headed. A life of discipleship will therefore mean that his followers must walk as Jesus has walked, displaying the same attitude, embracing the same risks, and energized with the same motivation.

Peter challenges Jesus' statement with a rebuke (8:32), the content of which we are not told, though Matt 16:22 is more explicit: "Never, Lord! This shall never happen to you!" (NIV). For Peter, Jesus' words are not congruent with the traditional consensus concerning the status of Messiah. He cannot reconcile Jesus' exalted status with his prediction of shameful

---

7. A group's "court of reputation" is defined by deSilva (*Hope of Glory*, 4–8, 27) as those persons (usually another group) whose opinions are significant for the establishment of the group's honor. Usually, in situations where the dominant culture is antagonistic, "supra-social entities" (e.g., God, Reason, or Nature) are invoked as the highest possible court, legitimating the identity and honor of the minority group.

suffering, and is concerned that Jesus is not giving himself enough honor. Jesus responds to the challenge with a counter-rebuke (8:33), in which he maintains the truth of his previous statement and demonstrates insight into Peter's challenge. He denigrates Peter's challenge by associating him with Satan, and contrasts the divine and human "courts of reputation," saying that Peter has regard to "human things" not "divine things." In other words, it is a diabolical attitude to set one's mind on human judgments rather than on God's.

The "self-denial" saying (8:34) maintains this emphasis of Jesus on the need for disciples to relinquish their regard for the worldly "court of reputation" (i.e., "man," "Satan," "self") and to identify with Jesus in his regard for the alternative (divine) "court of reputation," embracing the dishonor which will come to him from the worldly "court." In 8:35 the saving and losing of life is relativized according to the cause for which one saves or loses it. Loss of life "on account of me and the gospel" is an honorable loss in the eyes of the higher court, and is redefined paradoxically as the saving of life.

The idea of "profit" (equivalent to "advantage," comprising security and honor)[8] is the central concern of 8:36 and 37. Worldly gain is relativized by the consideration of heavenly gain, which, while implicit here, is made more explicit in verse 38. The worldly "court of reputation" is strongly castigated by the ascription "adulterous and sinful generation." Those who have regard to the honor bestowed by such a court are those who will have been "ashamed of me and my words," and these will miss out on the bestowal of divine honor (the Son of Man in the glory of the Father with the holy angels) in the future.

The Voice from Heaven Honors Jesus

Since radical self-denial and the possibility of death are weighty matters, potential disciples need to be assured that Jesus is really who he claims to be. In the transfiguration scene that follows (Mark 9:2–8), the setting is an auspicious one, a high mountain. The radiance and exceeding whiteness of Jesus' garments—"dazzling white, such as no one on earth could bleach them" (9:3)—are clear representations of divine honor. Moses and Elijah, much revered figures from the past, converse with Jesus (9:4). As Peter recognizes (9:5), Jesus is at least equal in honor to this company. The voice of God from the cloud (9:7, echoing Mark 1:11) is, for the disciples, a strong

8. deSilva, *Hope of Glory*, 15–16.

affirmation of the ultimate honorable identity of Jesus: he is Son of God, beloved of God, and the new prophet whose words, carrying the authority of the Father, are to be listened to.

As this material is arranged, then, in all three Synoptic Gospels, Jesus' foundational principles of discipleship are seen in the context of Christology. Peter's identification of Jesus (Mark 8:29) is modified by the prediction of suffering and death (8:31) and expanded by the affirmation of divine sonship (9:7). The demands of discipleship are consequent upon this revelation of Jesus' true identity and mission. The call to discipleship is not a call to an ideology or system of teaching or specific practices, but to the person of Jesus himself. The call to self-denial is a call to walk in his footsteps. The whole passage brings into bold contrast the exalted status of Jesus and the future dishonor he will suffer. The disciples are challenged to identify with Jesus in this shame, realizing that the world's verdict is not the only possible one.

THE SELF-DENIAL SAYINGS
IN MATTHEW'S GOSPEL

I mentioned above that the "self-denial" sayings are reported also by both Matthew and Luke. Both Matthew and Luke keep the sayings together and in the same order (Matt 16:24–25 and Luke 9:23–24). In addition, both Matthew and Luke present alternative forms of the same sayings (Matt 10:38–39 and Luke 14:27; 17:33) without the phrase "let them deny themselves," suggesting that these versions had a common origin in the source Q.[9] The Gospel of John also attests these two sayings, but in a modified form and in reversed order (John 12:25–26). Thus each of the two sayings has six formulations:

Mark	Matthew	Luke	John
8:34	16:24	9:23	12:26
8:35	16:25 10:38 10:39	9:24 14:27 17:33	12:25

9. The Q tradition is cited also in the Gospel of Thomas 55, an altered form of Matt 10:38.

Then Jesus told his disciples, "If any want to come after me, let them deny themselves and take up their cross and follow me. For those who want to save their life will lose it and those who lose their life for my sake will find it" (Matt 16:24–27).

Matthew seems to have used Mark's sayings with only minor changes.[10] He breaks the "save/lose" parallelism by introducing "find." (He uses the same word in a consistent "find/lose" parallelism in 10:39.) The grammatical changes in 16:26 are greater, but Matthew has merely reconstructed the rhetorical questions to avoid the use of infinitives. His adjustment of the next saying is more significant:

> For the Son of Man is to come in the glory of his Father with his angels and then he will repay everyone for what has been done. (Matt 16:27)

Here Matthew omits the first part of Mark 8:38 ("for those who are ashamed of me . . .) probably because a similar saying has been given in 10:33 (=Luke 12:8, 9—see below for discussion of this passage) where the language of confession and denial is used instead of the language of shame. The negative motivation of shame in Mark is replaced here by a positive expectation of eschatological reward, using the proverbial expression found also in Ps 62:12 and Prov 24:12—"You repay to all according to their work." The implication is that this time of divine reward is the ultimate goal of discipleship, the moment in which followers of Jesus "find" the eternal dimension of the life they have refused to "forfeit." The prospect of eschatological honor thus functions as a motivation for self-denial.

There may be a possible objection at this point: the idea of rewards for self-denial may seem to be ultimately self-serving, as if the sole reason for denying oneself in this life is to obtain honors for oneself in the next. However, it needs to be acknowledged that (a) Christian self-denial is done not for the sake of the benefits but for the sake of a person, and (b) a relationship of honor is not unilateral but reciprocal.[11]

The Literary Setting (Matt 16:13—17:8) as Honor Discourse

Matthew's redaction of the passage maintains the tenor of Mark's. After Peter's christological confession (16:16) that names Jesus not only as Christ

---

10. I am assuming Markan priority.

11. See Milbank, "Ethics of Self-Sacrifice."

but as "the Son of the living God," Jesus responds by granting honor to Peter. He does this by blessing him (16:17), by honorably renaming him (16:18), and by bestowing authority, symbolized by "the keys of the kingdom" (16:19). In this grant of honor Jesus makes a strong distinction between the realms of earth and heaven. "Flesh and blood" is contrasted with "my Father in heaven" (16:17), and the binding and loosing happens both on earth and in heaven; these are the two "courts of reputation," which are contrasted as "human things" and "divine things" in 16:23.

As noted above, Mark's appeal to the fear of eschatological shame is replaced in Matthew by the expectation of divine judgment (16:27). Although this is a more general concept, it is nevertheless one in which God's evaluation of each person (as either honorable or shameful) will be made public. In the transfiguration account, Matthew adds that Jesus' face "shone like the sun" (17:2), a description that strengthens the association with Moses. He also adds "with him I am well pleased" to the words of the voice from heaven (17:5); this is language that can encode the patron-client relationship—Jesus finds unique favor in the eyes of God. It seems clear, then, that Matthew's use of the "self-denial" sayings in their larger literary setting makes no less appeal to considerations of honor than does the Gospel of Mark.

Alternative Forms of the Sayings in Matt 10:38–39

> Whoever does not take up the cross and follow me is not worthy of me. Those who find their life will lose it, and those who lose their life for my sake will find it. (Matt 10:38–39)

As I indicated above, these alternative forms of the sayings are from a non-Markan source, and are used in quite different literary settings in both Matthew and Luke. Matthew places the alternative versions of both the "following" saying (Matt 10:38) and the "saving/losing" saying (Matt 10:39) in the context of Jesus' sending out of the Twelve (Matt 10:1—11:1). Luke's treatment of these versions (Luke 14:27 and 17:33) is discussed below.

The "following" saying in this form has no words corresponding to "deny oneself." It is expressed negatively; Matthew seems to have adapted the saying in the interests of parallelism with the language of "worthiness" in the preceding saying (10:37), which picks up the use of "worthy" from 10:11 and 10:13. This version of the "losing/saving" saying (10:39) has a simplified construction, using aorist participles. As in 16:25, Matthew uses the "finding" of life as a synonym for salvation for those who have lost their lives for Jesus' sake.

The Literary Setting (Matt 10:1–42) as Honor Discourse

These alternative versions of the sayings form part of Jesus' instructions to the Twelve. The chapter is full of the language of conflict, honor, and shame. The disciples must identify those who are "worthy," that is, those who welcome them (11–12a), and the "unworthy" will be negatively judged by the divine court (12b–15). But the disciples who follow Jesus will be negatively judged by the worldly court of reputation—the "wolves" include councils and synagogues, kings and governors, and all kinds of family members (16–21, 34–37). The persecution will include shameful behavior: flogging, betrayal by family members, hatred, verbal abuse, and there is even the possibility of death (21, 28). Disciples will endure this shame on account of Jesus (18, 22). A specific appeal to the teacher-disciple relationship is made in verses 24 and 25: dishonor suffered by the teacher is appropriately shared also by his disciples who follow him.

However, Jesus says four times, "Do not fear," and gives four reasons. First, faithful disciples will be allied with the highest (divine) court, evidenced by the help of the Spirit (19, 20). Second, there will be an eschatological reversal in which the hidden things will be revealed (26). Third, fear of bodily mistreatment is relativized by regard for the soul, which it is the prerogative of God to destroy, along with the body (28). Fourth, the disciples are of great value to the Father (29–31).

Jesus thus encourages the commissioned disciples as they face their predicted suffering; their endurance will be rewarded with salvation (22). But he also warns them. The "following" saying (10:38) plays its part here in sharpening the distinction between groups of people who are "worthy" and "unworthy." The "unworthy" are those who do not receive the gospel and its missionaries, and who do not support them (11–15), those who are attached to family more than to Jesus (37), those who publicly deny Jesus (33), and those who do not take up their cross and follow him (38), being fixated on constructing their own lives (39). Jesus' speech boils down to this: those who don't honor Jesus and his followers will not be honored by him. Conversely, the "worthy" who honor the gospel and its messengers will receive rewards as tokens of honor (40–42). Here again it's clear that a consideration of honor motivates self-denial.

THE SELF-DENIAL SAYINGS IN LUKE'S GOSPEL

Luke, like Matthew, seems to have used Mark's couplet of self-denial sayings, retaining its form and context but making several modifications. Luke writes that Jesus gave this teaching to "all," which must refer at least to the disciples, but probably includes Mark's "crowd" (Mark 8:34). Luke has a characteristic concern for the universality of the gospel, that is, *everyone* should know what it means to become a disciple.

> Then he said to them all, "If any want to come after me, let them deny themselves and take up their cross daily and follow me." (Luke 9:23)

Luke has added the words *kath hēmeran* to Mark's text, making the activity of "taking up the cross" a "daily" characteristic of Christian discipleship. With this metaphor, Luke seems to be urging followers of Jesus to identify with his suffering, to accept the risks and dangers that are the direct consequences of living as a committed disciple, and to resolve "to live on a daily basis as though one had been sentenced to death by crucifixion."[12] It is equivalent to "setting one's face" resolutely to follow Jesus (cf. Luke 9:51), thereby "putting one's head on the chopping block."[13]

> For those who want to save their life will lose it, and those who lose their life for my sake (they) will save it. (Luke 9:24)

Luke, like Matthew, has deleted Mark's phrase "and the gospel." The motivation for losing one's life is now expressed as solely on account of Jesus; this change has the effect of intensifying the christological focus. Luke's second modification adds a demonstrative pronoun (*houtos*) before the final verb, with the effect of putting more emphasis on the prospect of future salvation than on loss of life. The saying clearly announces a reward for those who set themselves on the road of radical discipleship for Jesus' sake. Jesus continues to explain in the next two verses what it means to preserve or lose one's life.

12. Green, *Gospel of Luke*, 372–73.

13. Nolland, *Luke 9:21—18:34*, 482. Luke may have had in mind the deaths of Stephen (Acts 6:8—8:1) and James (Acts 12:1–2).

> What does it profit them if they gain the whole world, but lose or
> forfeit themselves? (Luke 9:25)

Luke has substituted "themselves" for Mark's "their life," implying the
equivalence of the terms. His addition of "lose" where Mark only has "forfeit" helps to link the saying with the previous one. He has, however, deleted
Mark 8:37, "For what can they give in return for their life?"

> Those who are ashamed of me and of my words, of them the Son
> of Man will be ashamed when he comes in his glory and the glory
> of the Father and of the holy angels. (Luke 9:26)

Here Luke has eliminated Mark's phrase "in this adulterous and sinful generation" (Mark 8:38) but it appears later in 9:41. He has also adjusted the
saying to express the fact that the Son of Man (Jesus himself in his eschatological manifestation) has his own glory; this makes a strong connection to
the transfiguration passage immediately following, where the disciples see
his glory (9:32) and hear the voice of the Father (9:35).

A related Q saying, Luke 12:8, 9 (=Matt 10:32, 33), clarifies the expression of shame in this verse, using the language of denial (*arneomai*, to say
no) and its antonym in this context, confession (*homologeō*, to say yes):

> Everyone who confesses me before others, the Son of Man will
> confess also before the angels of God, but whoever denies me be-
> fore others will be denied before the angels of God. (Luke 12:8, 9)

Luke's form of this saying relates it to 9:26 by referring to "the angels of
God" rather than to Matthew's "my Father in heaven." To be ashamed of
Jesus and his words is to refuse to "confess" him, that is, to give him public honor. Here shame, the fear of human disapproval, motivates denial of
Jesus. The fear of *divine* disapproval, however, relativizes the power of this
shame, and motivates the public acknowledgement of Jesus.[14] The "confession" of Jesus involves the "denial" of self—the bearing of consequences
that might be seen by others as shameful. Later we'll consider what "being
ashamed of Jesus" might look like in practical terms.

---

14. Johnson, *Gospel of Luke*, 197. In the subsequent passages Luke maintains the
theme of the relativization of earthly possessions by the value of the heavenly (Luke
12:13–48).

An Alternative Form in Luke 14:27

Whoever does not carry their (own) cross and follow me cannot
be my disciple. (Luke 14:27)

Just as Matthew has alternative forms of the sayings we have now examined
in all three Synoptic Gospels, so does Luke. Luke 14:27 is an alternative
form of the "following" saying. This verse and its parallel in Matt 10:38
(see above) are probably derived from the Q tradition. While this form
has no explicit reference to "denying oneself" the concept is present in the
preceding verse (14:26, which we'll consider later), referring to the "hating"
of even one's own life.[15] Self-denial, along with family denial and "carrying
one's own cross" (and, in Luke 14:33, renunciation of all possessions) is thus
made the *sine qua non* of discipleship. Although Luke uses the pronoun *heauton* here (as in the previous verse) to strengthen the personal application
of the disciple's cross-bearing, there is nothing to suggest that "one's own
cross" is anything but participation in the sufferings specific to Christian
discipleship.

The Literary Setting (Luke 14:1–35) as Honor Discourse

The chapter in which we find this "following" saying is full of the language
of honor and shame. The narrative begins at a meal in a Pharisee's house.
Noticing how the guests were seeking places of honor, Jesus gives an explicit lesson in humility (14:7–10), affirming the honoring of the humble
but anticipating the eschatological humbling of those who exalt themselves
(14:11–14). Then comes the parable about the dinner invitees who made
excuses (14:15–24). In the context of Jesus' invitation to the kingdom, such
preoccupation with one's own possessions and relationships constitutes a
refusal to deny oneself and to honor the host.

In the next section (14:25–35) Jesus appears to be attempting to re-
duce the size of the "great multitudes" who are accompanying him (14:25).
His teaching, which includes the "following" saying (14:27), makes two
points. First, discipleship has a high cost, involving counter-cultural attitudes—disattachment from family and "self" (26), cross-bearing (27),
renunciation of possessions (33), and consequently the loss of sources of
worldly honor. Second, recognizing that the cost of discipleship is great,

---

15. See below on John 12:25 for the use of "hate" as a Semitic term of disattachment
rather than of emotion.

Luke provides a motivation to wholeheartedness (14:28–32). This motivation involves shame. Those who do make the commitment of discipleship will face public shame if they are not able to maintain their commitment. This kind of shame is exemplified in the similitude about the tower-builder who has insufficient resources to complete the construction (28–30). The result is ridicule, that is, public dishonor. Such ridicule and humiliation of a half-hearted and unsuccessful disciple would bring dishonor both to Jesus and to the gospel. Hence the very stringent prerequisites for discipleship expressed in this pericope. The subsequent similitude about the king who has to seek a truce because he realizes that his army is not strong enough (31–32) underlines the importance of counting the cost of discipleship.

Jesus seems to be clarifying the implications of the choices facing potential followers: there is shame for disciples (shame that Jesus elsewhere encourages disciples to embrace) but a different shame for failed disciples (shame from which he seems to want to spare the crowd). This rhetoric constitutes an argument from *pathos,* appealing to fear and avoidance of shame. It is clinched by a parable that compares such failed disciples with tasteless salt (34–35). Being a disciple, like being salt, is ostensibly good and honorable (*kalos*), but failure to make the grade results in a shameful end—being thrown out.

An Alternative Form in Luke 17:33

> Those who seek to make their life secure will lose it, but those who lose it will keep it alive. (Luke 17:33)

Just as Luke 14:27 is an alternative form of the "following" saying, Luke 17:33 is an alternative form of the "saving/losing" saying. Luke's choice of words here reveals a clear distinction between two kinds of "saving" of life. For the first, Luke uses the verb *peripoieomai*, usually translated "keep" or "preserve"—this is, the maintenance of one's own security at all costs. The second verb (*zōogoneō*) seems to refer more definitely to the eschatological salvation in which life (*zōē*) will be eternal.[16] The ultimate motive for "losing one's life" (that is, "for my sake") is missing here, and is replaced by the more negative one of avoidance of personal destruction on "the day of the Son of Man" (26, 30).

16. Caba, "Lukan Parenesis," 58–62.

The Literary Setting (Luke 17:20–37) as Honor Discourse

This saying is found in Jesus' eschatological discourse (Luke 17:20–37). Jesus begins by taking his cue from the Pharisees' interest (17:20) in the coming of the kingdom of God. He redefines this event as judgment that will come "in the days of the Son of Man" (22, 24, 26, 30). The point he makes is that the presence of the kingdom is not discerned "by observation," that is, by visible markers. This is true for the Son of Man himself, for he is not recognized among them (21) and will be rejected by them (25).

Biblical examples from the stories of Noah (26, 27) and Lot (28, 29) serve as warnings that attachment to possessions (28, 31) and to heedless engagement in activities of this world (27, 28) will bring eschatological disaster. The normal activities of life in Noah's day concealed the imminence of the judgment that unexpectedly fell. The situation was similar in Lot's day, when Sodom was unexpectedly destroyed. Jesus applies the lesson to the time of his hearers, when nothing visible will distinguish which of "two" will be "taken" (30–35). The prospect of divine judgment, when Jesus is fully "revealed" (30), relativizes worldly pursuits, including material goods, which must be "things left behind" (31). Jesus therefore delivers an imperative, combined with a negative example: "Remember Lot's wife" (32). The reason can be deduced from verse 33: she tried to make her life secure by attachment to worldly pursuits. She turned back "to the things behind" (Gen 19:26), disregarding the warning (Gen 19:17), and lost her life.[17]

In Luke's context, self-denial is, implicitly, disattachment from these worldly things, in preparation for, and expectation of, "the day of the Son of Man." "Keeping life alive" depends again on the distinction between earthly and ultimate concerns, and some things must be "left behind." The implicit rhetorical appeal is to fear of judgment, and the implicit exhortation is to give attention to what really matters—the kingdom of God. The "courts of reputation" here are "this generation" (25) who reject Jesus, and God, who reveals him (30, by implication of the "divine passive").

---

17. Note the language of saving (*sōzō*) of life (*psychē*) in this story (Gen 19:17, LXX). Luke uses the expression *ta opisō* also in 9:62, "No one who puts a hand to the plow and looks back is fit for the kingdom of God." Paul also uses the expression: "forgetting *ta opisō* and straining forward to what lies ahead" (Phil 3:13).

THE SELF-DENIAL SAYINGS IN JOHN'S GOSPEL

> Those who love their life (*psychē*) lose it, and those who hate their life (*psychē*) in this world will keep it for eternal life (*zōē*). If any would serve me, let them follow me, and where I am, there also my servant will be. If any would serve me, the Father will honor them. (John 12:25, 26)

Jesus' words in John 12:25 and 26 (possibly derived from independent authentic forms of Jesus tradition) again demonstrate a link between self-denial and honor. Here the "following" saying and the "saving/losing" saying are reversed in order, and are cast in more typically Johannine language. In the context of John's narrative, Jesus has announced, "The hour has come in which the Son of Man is to be glorified," and has told the parable about the grain of wheat, which dies, yet bears much fruit. The obvious reference is to Jesus himself, and this carries over into the saying about losing and saving one's life (12:25), yet the context strongly suggests a universal application, because of the presence of Greeks in Jesus' audience (20), the drawing of *all* people to himself (32), and the use of the inclusive "whoever" in 12:26.[18]

John 12:25, the "saving/losing" saying, maintains the antithesis of the synoptic forms, and shares some of the vocabulary, but the "saving/losing" contrast is expressed here by "loving" and "hating." The ultimate loss is for those who "love their life in this world" but salvation is for those who "hate their life in this world." The word pair "love/hate" is a Semitic idiom denoting strong preference rather than emotion.[19] Love implies attachment, while hate implies disattachment—the choice to turn away from an unfavored alternative.[20]

The "saving" of life is expressed as "keeping it in eternal life." The eschatological perspective is made explicit here by contrasting "eternal life" with "this world," and by the use of *zōē* instead of *psychē*. The *psychē* is not lost, it is "kept" and transformed into the more enduring *zōē*, the life of God (John 1:4).

John 12:26 parallels the synoptic "following" saying. In this version ("Whoever serves me must follow me") the bare bones of the form are retained, with "serve me" replacing "come after me," but there is no reference

---

18. Caba, "Lukan Parenesis," 63–65; Lindars, *Gospel of John*, 427–28.

19. See Michel, "*Miseō*."

20. Malina and Rohrbaugh, *Social-Science Commentary*, 86–88. Cf. Luke 14:26, where "hate" is urged in a similar context of discipleship and cross-bearing.

to "denying oneself," for the concept has been dealt with in the previous verse. The reference to "taking up the cross" is replaced by the more personal reference to "where I am," but the cross is very much in focus here. The hour has come for Jesus to be glorified (12:23), and he will die like a grain of wheat (24), being "lifted up from the earth" (32, 33). "Follow me" is explained as the servant's being where Jesus is. In John 13:36 Jesus says, "Where I am going, you cannot follow me now, but you will follow later." Peter disagrees, and correctly interprets this "following" as the possibility of laying down his own life (37, 38); this is confirmed by John 21:18–19, where Jesus predicts that Peter's "following" of Jesus will lead to his own death. Before that, however, Peter will deny Jesus, not himself (12:38).

Being "where Jesus is" thus has also a future aspect, for Jesus later tells his disciples that he will receive them into the place he will have prepared for them, "that where I am, there you may be also" (14:3). Being "where Jesus is" is being "in the glory of the Father." This is clear from John 17:24—it is Jesus' desire that his followers (those whom the Father has given him) might be with him where he is, so that they might see his glory. Following Jesus, then, clearly means following him to death, and through death, to the place of honor in which the followers are received and in which the glory of Jesus is revealed. In 12:26 the following and serving of disciples are explicitly linked to honor from the Father—"the Father will honor him." In this Gospel, the Father is honored by Jesus (8:49), and the Son is to be honored by all, just as the Father is honored (5:23). As the Father would glorify Jesus (12:23, a "divine passive") so the Father will honor those who follow Jesus in the same walk.

The Literary Setting (John 12:20–33) as Honor Discourse

In John 12 Jesus' prediction of his own death is expressed (in contrast to the synoptic accounts) in purely positive terms: the "death" of the grain of wheat leads to the bearing of much fruit (12:24), his being "lifted up from the earth" leads to the drawing of all people (32), and his death is described as "being glorified" (23). In these ways, the ultimate shame from the perspective of the human "court" is redefined in terms of divine honor. This strategy of redefinition appears to be a feature of John's Gospel. Jerome Neyrey treats John 18–19 as honor discourse, showing how the author makes great use of irony, whereby Jesus' sufferings, ostensibly shameful from the human viewpoint, are given the verdict of honor from the divine viewpoint; despite being treated shamefully, Jesus stays in control at all times, maintaining his honor.[21] For those who serve and follow Jesus, there is also the specific promise of the Father's honor (26).[22]

The voice from heaven (28) functions in this passage as it does in the synoptic transfiguration passages (Mark 9:7; Matt 17:5; Luke 9:35) as an authoritative affirmation of Jesus' honorable status. Jesus confirms that the voice is not for his benefit, but for the hearers (30). It is the immediate, positive, divine answer to Jesus' prayer, "Father, glorify your name" (28), indicating Jesus' favor with God. Jesus does not seek his own glory (John 8:50), but exemplifies the attitude of discipleship that seeks God's glory through submission and service. A strong contrast is made in the subsequent passage, where those who do not confess Jesus are described as loving human glory (approval) rather than the glory (approval) of God (12:42–43).

Self-denial, then, according to this passage, is a radical disregard for one's temporal existence, in favor of a life of following Jesus. The prospect of a death like his is a distinct possibility, but the promise of future honor from God is a stimulus to serve and follow.

CONCLUSIONS

In all three Synoptic Gospels, the "self-denial" sayings share a common literary context. Their strong challenge toward identifying with Jesus and radically following him is supported by vividly drawn contrasts between two "courts of reputation"—the human, traditional one and the "heavenly" one that consists of the Father, the Son of Man, and those associated with them in their glory. Since the honor of the latter is obviously a higher honor, it must have a stronger claim on our allegiance. Self-denial thus appears to involve renouncing the traditional sources of honor and seeking the higher.

The use of variant forms of these sayings by Matthew, Luke, and John in different literary settings supports and extends this perspective. Jesus calls for a revaluation of one's self, and a reassessment of one's life, in the light of honor and shame.

Jesus' words constitute a daunting prospectus for would-be followers of Jesus. The requirements of discipleship are self-denial, whole-hearted allegiance to him, and a daily willingness to embrace loss of honor and the

21. Neyrey, "Despising the Shame," 113–37.

22. This recalls 1 Sam 2:30, "Those who honor me I will honor, and those who despise me will be lightly esteemed."

risk of violent death. The refusal of these requirements has dire eschatological implications. However, the content of the sayings lies near the center of Jesus' program of liberation and transformation for humanity. Committed, radical disciples of Jesus must seek freedom from preoccupation with themselves (image, honor, and worldly security) and from the bondage of adherence to social systems that prescribe ways of living that stifle eternal life. Only those who unreservedly follow Jesus, despite the shame of the cross, are really free.

In summary, we have found that, in these texts, self-denial is:

- the relativization of the value of one's temporal life
- the whole-hearted giving of oneself to following Jesus
- giving Jesus public honor by "confessing" him
- bearing the shame of the cross and of discipleship
- associated with disattachment from possessions and family
- associated with persecution, suffering, and the possibility of death

The foundations of, and motivations for, such self-denial include:

- the person of Jesus as the one to whom loyalty and honor is given
- the prospect of eschatological shame—the fear of divine disapproval
- the promise of eschatological rewards and honor from the Son and the Father
- the possibility of dishonor to the gospel as a result of half-heartedness

The next chapter looks beyond the specific sayings that we have examined so far and considers other aspects of Jesus' teaching that enrich our understanding of his concept of self-denial.

CHAPTER 2

Self-Denial in Other Teachings of Jesus

In addition to these "self-denial" sayings and their literary contexts, there is much other material in Jesus' teaching that relates more indirectly to self-denial, honor, and shame. We'll now explore a wider range of texts in the Gospels, which will enable us to construct a fuller picture of self-denial as taught by Jesus. We'll ask four questions. First, we'll focus on some of the material in which Jesus addresses the great concern some people had for the promotion and maintenance of their own honor; in other words, what was Jesus' attitude to *self-exaltation*? Next, we'll ask about Jesus' expectations regarding the possible *consequences* of self-denial for his followers. Then we'll inquire into the *motivations* Jesus gave for self-denial: on what basis were disciples asked to deny themselves? Finally, we'll focus on the *methods* Jesus employed to promote the attitudes of self-denial and to affirm those who would deny themselves.

SELF-EXALTATION: THE ANTITHESIS OF SELF-DENIAL

We have seen that, for Jesus, self-denial (saying *no* to oneself) is equivalent to "losing one's life"—renouncing one's life in this world. The opposite attitude (saying *yes* to oneself) would be attempting to "save one's life" by "making one's life secure" (Luke 17:33) or by seeking to "gain the whole world" (Mark 8:36)—an attitude of self-interest and self-promotion, even self-exaltation. If self-denial is the renunciation of worldly honor, the antithesis of self-denial would be the pursuit of worldly honor. This is an attitude on which Jesus has much to say in the Gospels.

Jesus' Subversion of the Quest for Honor

In the first-century Mediterranean cultures, as in most cultures, a concern to do the honorable thing was normal and natural. To establish and maintain the honor of one's person, reputation, and way of living was a good and legitimate goal. However, the pursuit of an honorable life can easily become corrupted by competition for honor—a preoccupation with the quest for status. When concern for honor becomes paramount, then love of honor and fame arises, and is perceived by others as conceit.[1] The status-seeker may resort to hypocrisy as a strategy to get honor, posturing to attract respect. In the Gospels this concern for honor is very evident in many of those who formed Jesus' audiences. These people show a great concern to clarify precisely who is to participate in the honor of salvation, and how. An unnamed person asks Jesus, "Will only a few be saved?" (Luke 13:23). The disciples ask a similar question: "Who then can be saved?" (Mark 10:26). The disciples apparently presume that children have no place in the kingdom of God, but Jesus tells them, "The kingdom of God belongs to such as these" (Mark 10:14). This is very evidently an issue of status and honor.

John's Gospel uses the word "glory" (*doxa*) for honor. Jesus notes that the religious leaders "accept glory from one another and do not seek the glory that comes from God" (John 5:44). Later, John observes that certain fearful believers refused to acknowledge Jesus publicly because "they loved human glory more than the glory of God" (12:43, cf. 7:18). Jesus, in contrast, does not seek his own glory from human beings (5:41; 8:50). Neither does he glorify himself: "If I glorify myself, my glory is nothing," for he obtains his honor from God (8:54).

We also see in Jesus' audiences a concern to be "first." His disciples discuss which of them is the greatest (Mark 9:34). Later, James and John request places of honor when Jesus comes into his glory (Mark 10:37). On several occasions Jesus challenges people (mostly Pharisees) whom he

---

1. Many writers in the ancient world were critical of those who were ambitious for honor, reputation, status, and fame. See Downing, "'Honor' among Exegetes," 63–66. The Old Testament, of course, is full of passages that castigate pride.

perceives to be exalting themselves (e.g., Matt 23:1–36 and parallels, Luke 16:14–15; 18:9–14).

Jesus' responses to perceptions or expressions of status-seeking can be seen as examples of his unique "subversive wisdom, which cuts against the prevailing conventional wisdom at every point."[2] No passage in the Gospels more powerfully illustrates the practice of self-denial than the parable of the "good Samaritan" (Luke 10:30–37), which is told for the benefit of a lawyer who wishes to "justify himself"—to be seen as fully righteous. The disturbing message of the story is that he should deny himself. Love for God and neighbor demands a disregard for one's standing in the community, one's ritual purity, and one's personal safety.[3]

Jesus' challenges to status-seeking are notable for the frequent reappearance of a small number of antithetical word-pairs, with the vocabulary overlapping somewhat in some passages. These are often expressed as paradoxes: first versus last, leader versus servant, exalting versus humbling, and sayings about children. Many of these responses are in the form of pronouncement stories, where the antithetical paradox comes at the end of the narrative.

The "First/Last" Sayings

In Mark 10:31 Jesus says, "Many who are first will be last, and the last first." This saying is used also by Matthew and Luke, but in different contexts. In Mark's Gospel it functions as a summing-up for the story of the rich man who came to Jesus wanting to inherit eternal life. Jesus' statement to him relativizes wealth: "Go, sell what you own and give to the poor, and you will have treasure in heaven, then come, follow me." But the man is unwilling. Jesus continues to explain to the disciples that his followers will be rewarded when they renounce houses and kindred. The conclusion of the story is that many of those who are regarded as "first" in this world (implying those who have property and families, and thus status and security) will, in the perspective of eternity, actually be "last," and *vice versa*. Jesus overturns the

---

2. Wright, *Jesus and the Victory*, 315.

3. Bailey's treatment of the parable (*Through Peasant Eyes*, 33–56) illuminates the implications of honor in the actions of the characters. For example, the victim is stripped of all that would mark him as worthy to be aided; the priest is unwilling to suffer the humiliation of ritual impurity; the Levite is unwilling to affront his superior by not following his example; but the Samaritan lays aside his own agenda, places himself in personal danger and risks retaliation—his own honor is not his primary consideration.

conventional idea that wealth is a sign of good standing with God; in fact, it is a hindrance to entering the kingdom of God.

Matt 20:16 uses the same "first/last" saying as a very literal summing-up (in a temporal sense) of the parable of the laborers in the vineyard. Here the "first" are those who have worked hardest and longest, and the "last" are those who have hardly begun, but Jesus overturns the conventional expectation that rewards are commensurate with labor. Instead, the master of the house who is "good" does what is "right" and bestows his favor on all the workers equally, beginning with those who were hired last. The least worthy receive the greater grace.

Luke 13:30 concludes a parable that is clearly addressed to the people of Israel who expect to be let in to the kingdom of God. However, the master of the house says to them, "I do not know where you are from." Jesus predicts their exclusion. Then, ironically, foreigners who come from all directions are accepted to recline at table in the kingdom, no matter "where they are from"! Jesus thus reverses the conventional notion that those of Israel are "insiders" with guaranteed status in God's eyes—the "first" are again "last," and the "last" are "first."

The "Leader/Servant" Sayings

There is a group of sayings that deals with reversal of rank. In God's kingdom, there is a restructuring of roles: those who are ambitious for leadership become servants, and those who faithfully serve receive great honor. In Mark 10:43–44 (paralleled in Matt 20:26–27) Jesus says, "Whoever wants to become great among you, must be your servant, and whoever wants to be first among you, must be the slave of all." In Mark and Matthew this saying is placed directly after Jesus' third passion prediction. James and John request places of honor for themselves. There is considerable irony here: having just heard Jesus' prediction of his humiliation, they are concerned for their own exaltation! In response (Mark 10:42) Jesus makes reference to the rulers of the Gentiles who "lord it over" them and "exercise authority over" them. Jesus strongly disapproves of this attitude among his disciples—those who aspire to become "great" or "first" are to be, paradoxically, servants (*diakonos*) or slaves (*doulos*).

The thrust of the sayings is different from that of the "first/last" sayings discussed above. There, Jesus addresses those who presume they are "first"—they will be made "last." Here, Jesus addresses those who *want* to be "great/first"—they are to *make themselves* servants and slaves, following the example of Jesus (Mark 10:45; John 13:14). The idea of "wanting to be great" need not indicate selfish ambition. The word "great" (*megas*) is a term of esteem, used of Jesus (Luke 1:32) and John the Baptizer ("great before the Lord," Luke 1:15). The word for "first" (*prōtos*) here has the sense of "leader," as it does in Mark 6:21, Luke 19:47, and Acts 13:50. Although the word refers to an honorable rank, there seems to be more emphasis on function here. Luke makes this more explicit in his parallel passage, substituting the more specific *hēgoumenos* (leader) for *prōtos* (Luke 22:26).

This group of sayings reaffirms Jesus' call to self-denial through the voluntary acceptance of the lowly status of a servant or slave. He illustrates the attitude he is asking for with his own example: the Son of Man is certainly to be thought of as a ruler and a leader—he is, after all, the Christ, but he came to serve (*diakoneō*) and to give his life (Mark 10:45).

Luke's version, placed in the narrative of the last Passover supper, uses additional metaphors: "The greatest among you must become like the youngest, and the leader like one who serves" (Luke 22:26). Moreover, as Jesus says of himself, contrary to all convention, the one who serves is greater than the one who reclines at the table (Luke 22:27).

Mark 9:35b is another version of the saying: "Whoever wants to be a leader must be last of all and servant of all." This is an expanded form of Mark 10:43, which was discussed above. It occurs as part of Jesus' response to the disciples' discussion about who among them is greatest (Mark 9:33–37 = Matt 18:1–5 = Luke 9:46–48). Luke's version (Luke 9:48) identifies "the least among all of you" as the one who is "great."

Matthew provides a saying using language that overlaps with the "humbling" and "children" groups of sayings: "Whoever becomes humble like this child is the greatest in the kingdom of heaven" (Matt 18:4). In this literary context, all three synoptists link the sayings about greatness with sayings about children (see below). Matthew 23:11 is another instance of the saying, this time with the antithetical terms "greatest" and "servant"— "The greatest among you will be your servant." It appears in conjunction with the "exalting/humbling" saying (examined in the next section), not in a narrative context, but embedded in a long passage in which woes are proclaimed to the Pharisees.

These "leader/servant" sayings express a complete reversal of the cultural values placed on rulers and slaves. Jesus' disciples are to follow him in renouncing the ways of the great ones of this world, with their concern for power and honor, and instead, taking on the role of those who serve. In doing so, they will be "great" in God's eyes, for God is the one who grants honor (Matt 20:23), and he is the higher and more worthy benefactor (Luke 22:25).

John's Gospel has none of these "leader/servant" sayings, but Jesus demonstrates his own teaching in washing the disciples' feet (John 13:1–17). Though he has an exalted status, he humbles himself, taking the form of a servant, as Paul puts it in Phil 2.

The "Exalting/Humbling" Sayings

The Gospel writers report that Jesus said, "Those who exalt themselves will be humbled, and those who humble themselves will be exalted." This saying is used by Matthew and Luke only, in contexts that are distinctly their own. In each case the saying functions as a strong castigation of self-promotion. Jesus did not introduce this as a novel idea, for the reversal of roles between proud and humble was well attested in Greco-Roman literature and practice.[4]

Matt 23:12, together with the previous verse (a form of the "leader/ servant" saying), is included in Matthew's long compilation of material in which Jesus condemns the attitudes of the hypocritical scribes and Pharisees (Matt 23:1–39). In verses 5–7 Matthew uses material in common with Mark 12:38–40 and Luke 20:45–47. This material is a catalogue of conceit:

> They do everything in order to be seen by people, making their phylacteries broad and their fringes long. They like to walk around in long robes, and for the sake of appearance say long prayers. They love places of honor at banquets, seats of honor in the synagogues, respectful greetings in the marketplaces, and people calling them Rabbi. (Matt 23:5–7)

Those who exalt themselves like this, says Jesus, will be humbled, presumably by God.[5] In contrast, the saying urges disciples to "humble themselves." The use of the pronoun "themselves" (*heauton*) recalls the "self-denial" saying ("deny themselves," Mark 8:34), while the antithetical parallelism of the

4. See Balch, "Rich and Poor." The lifting up of the lowly and the bringing down of the proud is a common theme in the Old Testament, e.g., 1 Sam 2:7; Ps 75:7; Isa 2:11; Ezek 17:24; 21:26.

5. In Mark 12:40 and Luke 20:47 they will "receive greater condemnation," which Matt 23:33 specifies as "being sentenced to hell."

form recalls the "saving/losing" saying (Mark 8:35). The call to humility here is implicitly a call to serve others, for over-attention to self obviously entails neglect of others.

Luke 14:11 uses the "exalting/humbling" saying in the same form, except that participles replace the verbs. The saying concludes a teaching of Jesus (Luke 14:7–11) that Luke calls a parable. The topic is, very explicitly, honor and shame. Observing the status-seeking behavior of guests at a sabbath meal, Jesus advises them not to seek the place of honor but the lowest place. The motivation for this is, first, the avoidance of shame, in the case that a person may be demoted to a place of lesser honor, and secondly, the possibility of public honor, in the case that the person may be promoted to a position of greater prestige. Jesus makes a difference between exalting oneself (acting on the presumption of one's honorable status) and the legitimate acceptance of honor bestowed by another. Jesus' strategy does not advocate false humility, but provides opportunities for the giving and receiving of honor.[6] The "exalting/humbling" saying, then, functions as a very literal summary of the story. In this setting, to humble oneself is clearly to take voluntarily a position of lower status—to renounce one's claim to honor of one kind (self-perceived) while opening oneself to honor of another kind (freely bestowed).

Luke 18:14 includes the same saying in the same form, again functioning as the pithy punchline of the parable of the Pharisee and the tax collector (Luke 18:9–14). This story is directed to Pharisees, as in Matthew's setting of the saying. Luke tells us that the audience consists of "some who trusted in themselves that they were righteous, and regarded others with contempt" (18:9). The posture and prayer of the Pharisee vividly depict the attitude of self-exaltation: he stands and recites his own exceptional observance of Torah, taking a high view of himself and a low view of all others. The posture and prayer of the tax collector likewise demonstrates humility: standing with eyes lowered in shame, "at a distance" because of his uncleanness and unworthiness, he acknowledges the poverty of his claims to God's favor. There is an implicit divine verdict at the end of the story—the despised and lowly tax collector goes home "justified"; God has honored him by declaring him righteous; the humble one has been exalted. The implication is that if the self-righteous Pharisee should renounce his bloated

6. The subsequent section (Luke 14:12–14) illustrates the same thing, but from the point of view of the gracious host, who is urged to forsake the conventional reciprocity of honor transactions (i.e., invitations in return) by inviting those of low status. In doing so, the host is pronounced "blessed" and is promised divine eschatological honor.

ego and wholeheartedly say *no* to himself, he would avoid his (understated) enforced humiliation at the hands of God.

The Sayings about Children

On two recorded occasions Jesus takes the opportunity provided by the presence of children to make points about the kingdom of God. One of these is the occasion mentioned above, in which the disciples argue about who is the greatest (Mark 9:33–37; Matt 18:1–5; Luke 9:46–48). Here Jesus takes a child as an object lesson. On the other occasion, unnamed people, probably mothers, bring babies to Jesus for a blessing, but the disciples rebuke them; in response, Jesus makes further pronouncements using the analogy of children (Mark 10:13–16; Matt 19:13–15; Luke 18:15–17). These sayings about children do not have the form of the other groups of sayings, with their paradoxical and antithetical language. Nevertheless, they function in a similar way, as strong challenges in which Jesus counters the attitude of the disciples.

There appears to have been much textual borrowing, and perhaps some harmonization, between these similar passages. The sayings fall into three groups, each making a related point.

(a) Receiving Children

Mark 9:37a says, "Whoever receives one such child in my name receives me." Children are to be received in Jesus' name, and such a welcome is equivalent to receiving Jesus. This point is applied to the question of who is the greatest (also in Matt 18:5 and Luke 9:48). In this setting, the disciples are concerned about "greatness," that is, about status, leadership, and honor. In a status-based system, one sees no need to welcome persons of lower rank—deference is due only to those higher up. Jesus, however, insists that they must welcome even such people as children. Although Judaism in the first century assigned a higher value to children than did the Greco-Roman world generally, the social status of children was low, similar to that of the poor, marginalized, and exploited members of society.[7] Mark makes Jesus' lesson with the child a sequel to the "first/last" saying (Mark 9:35); the child, then, is an example of one who is "last of all, and servant of all." Luke,

---

7. Spitaler, "Welcoming a Child," 429n15; Francis, *Adults as Children*, 95.

at the conclusion of his version of the incident, includes the words "for the one who is least among all of you, this one is great" (Luke 9:48). Matthew's version adds another saying, in which the child becomes a symbol of humility: "Those who humble themselves as this child, they are greatest in the kingdom of heaven" (Matt 18:4); the sense is not that the child has humbled itself, but that the disciples must humble themselves even to the lowliness of the child. This is clarified by Matt 18:3—the disciples must "change and become like children."

(b) The Kingdom Belongs to Children

In Mark 10:14 Jesus says, "Let the little children come to me. Do not stop them, for it is to such as these that the kingdom of God belongs." The kingdom of God "belongs to" children; this point is applied to the disciples' rebuke of the mothers (Mark 10:14; Matt 19:14; Luke 18:16). The reason for the rebuke is not given, but Jesus' response implies that the disciples were turning away rightful heirs of the kingdom, making judgments about the worthiness of those desiring Jesus' favor. Jesus makes it clear that the kingdom belongs to those who, like children, are without claim or merit; it is not a matter of status achieved, but of grace bestowed and received.

(c) Receiving the Kingdom "as a Child"

In the next verse, Mark 10:15, Jesus says, "Whoever does not receive the kingdom of God as a little child will never enter it." This point is applied in slightly different ways in both literary settings (here and in Luke 18:17, cf. Matt 18:3, 4). The phrase "as a little child" (*hōs paidion*) is ambiguous because it is not clear whether *paidion* is in the nominative or accusative case. If it is nominative, the verse means that we should receive the kingdom "like a child receives the kingdom."[8] What characteristics of children might Jesus be referring to here? Many have been suggested,[9] but the thrust of the settings and of the other associated sayings makes it most plausible that Jesus is using the child as a model of one who has no basis for pretensions of greatness—those who are of such low status that they can do

8. E.g., Francis, "Children and Childhood," 66–72; Evans, *Mark 8:27—16:20*, 94; Nolland, *Luke 9:21—18:34*, 882.

9. Nolland (*Luke 9:21—18:34*, 882) suggests openness, willingness to trust, freedom from hypocrisy or pretension, conscious weakness, and readiness for dependence.

nothing but receive, openly and confidently, what is given.[10] However, if *paidion* is accusative, the child is passive, not active, and the verse means that we should receive the kingdom as we would receive a child, that is, in the same way as Jesus has welcomed the children.[11] The child, in this case, is a model of those who are welcomed, received, and blessed by God—that is, those of low status. "The disciples must act like adults, not like children, and demonstrate hospitality toward persons whose status they do not share."[12] Matthew's version is different, and more specific: it states that "unless you change and become like children you will never enter the kingdom of heaven" (Matt 18:3). He identifies the critical attitude of childlikeness as humility (18:4).

In both settings, the disciples are concerned about status, and in both settings, Jesus overturns this concern, placing greater value on the receiving of grace. The child is positively affirmed in its humility and low status, and in its lack of concern for status, and Jesus himself identifies with this lowliness. The message for the disciples is that, in order to enjoy favor with God, all claims to achievement must be abandoned. Followers of Jesus must deny their aspirations to worldly esteem; they must humble themselves, and accept loss of status for the sake of the kingdom.

In all these sayings, in which Jesus denounces self-exaltation and demands humility, he is redefining the conventional notions of social status and precedence. For those who are perceived as "last" in the human "court of reputation" there is a new verdict: they are "first" in the divine perspective. For those who "humble themselves" there is the promise of divine honor: God will exalt them. For those who take the role of the servant or slave there is a new designation: they are "great" in God's eyes. Those who renounce the quest for honor, welcome those of low status, and themselves become "as children" find that this is the only way to enter the kingdom of God.

---

10. Lane, *Gospel According to Mark*, 340. Weren ("Children in Matthew," 53–63) comments that because children occupy the lowest position in society, to be "as children" is to break with the conventional hierarchy of values and opt for a life that is characterized by vulnerability.

11. Moeser, *Anecdote in Mark*, 224–28; Spitaler, "Welcoming a Child." Spitaler's paper is persuasive, providing an impressive structural analysis of the literary context to clarify the figure's function. The construction is similar to that in Mark 12:31, "love your neighbor as yourself (*hōs seauton*)."

12. Spitaler, "Welcoming a Child," 425.

These sayings appear to function as a significant part of Jesus' attempts to challenge, stimulate, and motivate his disciples to "deny themselves." The obvious parallelism of these sayings with the "saving/losing" saying makes them supportive of Jesus' words about self-denial. He says, in effect, "Go ahead, deny yourself—take up the cross, lose your life, humble yourself, accept low status, be last, be a servant, be a child—for in doing so you will save your life, God will exalt you, give you high status, make you a leader, make you great."

THE CONSEQUENCES OF SELF-DENIAL

It has been said that Jesus' summons to deny oneself, take up the cross, and follow him "places him and his followers firmly on the map of first-century socially and politically subversive movements."[13] In other words, self-denial on account of Jesus is not a private spiritual exercise, nor is it denial of one's individuality—one's uniquely personal selfhood.[14] Rather, self-denial is an attachment to Jesus that relativizes all other attachments. It's a countercultural distancing of oneself from the approbation of one's society. It's a revaluation of social norms. It follows, then, that self-denial is an attitude toward self and society that necessarily has social consequences. There are strong indications in the Gospels that Jesus expected significant difficulties for his disciples, in the areas of family, wealth, and social standing, and that many of his followers actually experienced these.

Loss of Family

The first reference to a disruption of family relationships brought about by following Jesus is the passage that tells how Jesus' initial disciples Peter, James, and John left their trade and their household (Mark 1:16–20; Matt 4:18–22).[15] At the end of the story about the rich young ruler, found in all

13. Wright, *Jesus and the Victory*, 304.

14. Jesus' requirement for his followers to "love your neighbor as yourself" recognizes that it is natural for one to do good to or for oneself. From other texts it can be deduced that there is a legitimate kind of self-love that acknowledges one's worth and status before God.

15. These and other texts mentioned in this section are fully discussed in a masterful study by Barton, *Discipleship and Family Ties*. There were biblical precedents for leaving family: Ruth left her family and native land to come to Israel, and Abram, who left his

three Synoptic Gospels, Peter refers to this leaving, saying to Jesus, "Look, we have left everything and followed you" (Mark 10:28; Matt 19:27). In Luke's version Peter says, "Look, we have left our own (*ta idia*) and followed you" (Luke 18:28), implying that they have left their homes (cf. John 1:11), including both people and property. Jesus, in responding, affirms this "leaving." His list of things left behind includes house, brothers, sisters, mother, father, children, and farms (Luke conflates some of these terms, deletes farms, but includes wife). Kenneth Bailey points out the "radical rupture of the fabric of cultural loyalties" that Jesus' words create:

> The two unassailable loyalties that any Middle Easterner is almost required to consider more important than life itself are *family* and the *village home*. When Jesus puts both of these in *one* list, and then demands a loyalty that supersedes them both, he is requiring that which is truly impossible to the Middle Easterner, given the pressures of his culture.[16]

Yet Peter and the disciples claim to have done what the rich man in the story would not do—sell all his possessions, give to the poor, and follow Jesus. From the classic chiastic structure of the story, framed by references to "eternal life," we see that this "leaving" is the new form of obedience that is equivalent to the old commandments requiring respect for family, property, and parents, but that supersedes them.[17]

Matthew and Luke report two forms of a Q saying that relativizes family relationships: those who love father, mother, son, or daughter more than Jesus are "not worthy" of him (Matt 10:37). Luke uses the stronger language of "hate," in the sense of disattachment,[18] adding children and (again) wife,

kindred and his father's house in response to God's call, was held up as an example for all proselytes to Judaism. The Roman historian Tacitus wrote (*History*, 5:5): "Those who come over to their religion have this lesson first instilled into them, to despise all gods, to disown their country, and set at naught parents, children, and brothers." That is, a change of belief involved a change of community as well.

16. Bailey, *Through Peasant Eyes*, 169.

17. The chiasm is outlined in Bailey, *Poet and Peasant*, 53.

18. As noted above, the word pair "love/hate" is a Semitic idiom denoting strong preference rather than emotion. Love implies attachment, while hate implies disattachment, the choice to turn away from an unfavored alternative. Gen 29:30–34 states that Jacob loved Rachel more than Leah, who perceived that she was "hated" (not loved) but after she bore her third child she said, "Now at last my husband will become *attached* to me." In a collectivist society, attachment to a group is all-important, and disattachment is disaster. Love and hate express practical choices, not feelings. To love God with all one's heart means total attachment to him—total obedience to his ways. To love one's neighbor

and "even one's own life" (Luke 14:26). In requiring "hate" for family and self, Jesus is not calling his disciples to revile the family, to dishonor it, to rebel against it, or aim to disrupt it, for on other occasions he affirms the family.[19] Rather, he is calling them to make a practical choice, that is, to break their attachment to the family, because there is, for them, a higher loyalty, a more valuable attachment, a greater love. As noted previously, both these verses occur in conjunction with the "following" saying (Matt 10:38; Luke 14:27); they give the conditions for discipleship. As Stephen Barton notes,

> Discipleship of Jesus poses a threat to family and household ties, since it involves the disciple—every disciple—in a quite funda-mental transfer of primary allegiance and commitment.[20]

Jesus actually stands in solidarity with the attitude of Moses, who, in his blessing of Levi, relativizes the claims of kindred and allows formal and legal severance of family relationships for the sake of priestly duty to God:

> He said of his father and mother, "I have no regard for them." He did not recognize his brothers or acknowledge his own children, but he watched over Your word and guarded Your covenant. (Deut 33:9)[21]

A disciple's choice to follow Jesus is a choice to deny self—to relinquish one's social identity and status as defined by blood and marriage and family, and to accept a new identity and status defined by association with him. Jesus disallows the priority of family burial duties: "Let the dead bury their dead" (Matt 8:22; Luke 9:60). This is a scandalous disregard for the obligation, strongly held by both Greeks and Jews, to honor one's kin. Jesus claims, in effect, that loyalty to himself should take precedence over adherence to the household, relativizing the place of the family as a major Jewish cultural

means fulfilling one's duty to kinfolk and those in the village, because they are attached socially. Hating something or someone, then, means refusal to be attached; in practical social terms it may imply a cutting off of relationship, expulsion, and shunning. Cf. Mal 1:2f; Luke 16:13; John 12:25.

19. For example, he approves the fifth commandment (Matt 19:19) and the support of one's parents (Matt 15:4); he prohibits divorce (Matt 19:5, 31–32; 19:3–9); he uses family language (Abba, Father); he maintains a close relationship with his mother; his teachings contain positive family images (Luke 11:11–13; Luke 15).

20. Barton, *Discipleship and Family Ties*, 20.

21. Mayes, *Deuteronomy*, 403. This higher allegiance to YHWH legitimated the priests as agents of capital punishment of their kin, e.g., Exod 32:25–29; Num 25:8.

and religious symbol.[22] Thus, as Barton notes, the parting of Judaism and Christianity began at the mundane level of domestic relations and household ties.[23] N. T. Wright comments:

> In a world where family identity counted for a good deal more than in today's individualized western culture, the attitude Jesus was urging would result in the disciple effectively *denying his or her own basic existence* (emphasis mine).[24]

Other sayings in which family solidarity pales beside the message of the kingdom include the following:

- Mark 3:33–35 (Matt 12:48–50; Luke 8:21), in which Jesus leaves his family waiting outside while indicating that his present audience of disciples are "my mother and my brothers."

- Mark 6:4 (Matt 13:57; Luke 4:24), in which Jesus acknowledges that a prophet is without honor in his own household and among his own relatives.

- Luke 11:27–28, in which Jesus turns aside from an opportunity to direct honor to his mother, in favor of honoring those who hear and obey the word of God.

The subordination of family ties was a rhetorical theme in both Jewish and Greco-Roman traditions, and so the Gospel audiences would not have found it entirely new.[25] This suggests that the stark, categorical, and unconditional quality of many of Jesus' sayings on the topic of family is the result of a rhetorical aim—a deliberate use of hyperbole and metaphor for the purpose of pointedly driving home the importance and urgency of the task of proclaiming the reign of God, tied to Jesus' own preeminent role as Messiah. In view of this task, every obstacle is to be displaced.[26]

---

22. Wright, *Jesus and the Victory*, 398–403.

23. Barton, *Discipleship and Family Ties*, 222.

24. Wright, *Jesus and the Victory*, 402–3.

25. Barton, "Relativisation of Family Ties," 81–100; also Barton, *Discipleship and Family Ties*, 23–56. Barton notes references to the topic in Philo, Josephus, the Cynics, and the Stoics.

26. Barton, "Relativisation of Family Ties," 81.

Loss of Wealth

In the first century wealth was measured by possessions, primarily land, but also goods, family, and servants. The display of wealth was a symbol of honor and of social power. The Gospels, however, are unanimous in presenting wealth as a hindrance to discipleship.

In the parable of the sower, the "deception of wealth" is said to "choke the word" (Mark 4:19). In the story of the rich young ruler, Jesus comments to his disciples about how difficult it is for the rich to enter the kingdom of God (Mark 10:24–25). Their surprise at this saying (Mark 10:26) suggests an assumption on their part that the rich, obviously greatly favored by God, are sure to inherit the kingdom. Jesus' reversal of this perverted understanding of covenant blessing constitutes a sustained determination to relativize the value of worldly wealth by placing it over against the things God values. The parable of the rich man and Lazarus (Luke 16:19–31) is a graphic portrayal of this reversal—the rich man experiences suffering after death, while the poor man is comforted.

Matt 6:19–34 (= Luke 12:21–34) addresses this issue: anxiety about economic matters (food, drink, and clothing) is placed over against the love and provision of the Father (Matt 6:25–34; Luke 12:22–32) and the "treasures of earth" are compared unfavorably to "treasure in heaven" (Matt 6:19–21; Luke 12:21, 33–34). For Luke, money is one of the things highly esteemed by people (the Pharisees are "lovers of money") but "what people value highly is detestable in God's sight" (Luke 16:14–15 NIV); instead, Jesus urges consideration of the "true riches" (Luke 16:11).

To a man concerned about the division of his family inheritance, Jesus tells a story about a rich fool who plans, in conversation with himself, to hoard his goods and enjoy the pleasures of life (Luke 12:13–21). However, he finds that the riches he so greatly values are of no benefit to him on the night of his death. This parable provides a commentary on the "self-denial" sayings by illustrating the attitude of saying *yes* to oneself rather than *no*, and the ultimately unprofitable work of trying to "gain the whole world."

Wealth ("Mammon") is personified as a master competing with God (Matt 6:24; Luke 16:13); it is impossible to serve both masters. Thus, Jesus' relativization of wealth is equivalent to a "radicalization of the first commandment"[27]—idols cannot be tolerated if God reigns.

---

27. Wolff, "Humility and Self-Denial," 148, quoting G. Haufe.

However, this obligation to reject other gods has practical consequences: a choice must be made to "love one and hate the other" (Matt 6:24; Luke 16:13). This is a call for disattachment from wealth as a controlling factor in one's life. For this reason, Jesus presents to the rich young ruler an exacting condition for discipleship: "Go, sell your possessions, and give to the poor, and you will have treasure in heaven; then come, follow me" (Matt 19:21 and parallels). In the story, the disciples seem to have gone some way in fulfilling this condition, for Peter says, "Look, we have left everything and followed you" (Matt 19:27). Jesus promises a hundredfold return for those who leave family, homes, and lands for his sake (Matt 19:29). Metaphorical though this saying may be,[28] it is clear that Jesus honors the voluntary renunciation of those things that would constitute wealth in that culture.

In the same vein is Jesus' stringent requirement, "None of you can become my disciple if you do not give up all your possessions" (Luke 14:33; cf. Luke 12:33). Here the word for "give up" carries the sense of "saying goodbye" (cf. Mark 6:46; Luke 9:61). If this is not a call to literal disposal of property, it is certainly a call to abandonment of the right of ownership, with consequent dependence on God to supply all needs. The prayer for "daily bread" (Matt 6:11) expresses this dependence well.

A saying which promises a life of poverty, homelessness and itinerancy for disciples is Jesus' response to a scribe who asserts that he will follow Jesus wherever he goes: "Foxes, have holes, and birds of the air have nests, but the Son of Man has nowhere to lay his head" (Matt 8:20; Luke 9:58). Ironically, the Son of Man suffers greater deprivation than wild animals; his disciples can expect no less sense of poverty and dislocation. However, it is clear that Jesus does not call disciples to poverty for its own sake, but to a new kind of community.[29]

This brief overview of some of Jesus' sayings about wealth demonstrates that his call to "deny oneself and follow him" is equivalent to his call to "leave everything and follow him." Disattachment from money and possessions, like disattachment from family, seems to be the practical result of the attitude of self-denial. Jesus asks for total commitment, expressed in the currency of everyday life. Plato, the Stoics, and other philosophers had recognized the folly of maintaining a grasp on possessions, to the exclusion of what is of real and lasting value,[30] but for Jesus and the Gospel writers,

---

28. Exegetes argue about this; see May, "Leaving and Receiving."

29. Barr, "Eye of the Needle," 31–44.

30. Garrett, "Beloved Physician of the Soul?" 85–87. For a survey of Greco-Roman

the motivation for the relinquishment of wealth was rooted in the honor of the person of Jesus, and in the favor promised and already bestowed on disciples by God, as we will discover below.

This discussion has concentrated on voluntary, active relinquishment of wealth, because this is the thrust of the Gospel texts; the possibility of enforced poverty for disciples, perhaps as a result of family sanctions, is implied but not stated.[31] The consequences of such sanctions are referred to in the Tosefta: "One does not sell to them [those banned or excommunicated] or receive from them or take from them or give to them."[32] Such people would suffer a severe loss of wealth and social standing.

Persecution

Jesus foresees that the kind of self-denial demanded by radical discipleship will entail persecution (Mark 10:30 and parallels). He predicts (Matt 10:16–23; Mark 13:9–13) that his followers, in the context of their mission, will be "hated by all" and "handed over" for scourging and death, just as he himself will be. He expects that they will experience resistance, hostility, ostracism, and marginalization, and that the persecutors will include family members.

Matt 10:34–36 (= Luke 12:51–53) gives some indication of the possible consequences of a disciple's change of loyalties: the family may become hostile. Referring to Mic 7:1–7, Jesus states that he has come not to bring peace, but division; he anticipates that "one's enemies will be members of one's own household" (Matt 10:36). A plausible scenario might be as follows:[33] the family of a disciple is unwilling to suffer the shame of being associated with Jesus, and feel that they are being betrayed. The disciple is regarded as disloyal, perhaps even rebellious. The family is thus obliged to defy and discourage those who have "defected" to the new way, along the lines of Deut 21:18–21, which gives instructions for the treatment of "stubborn and rebellious sons," advising chastisement, seizure, trial, and stoning.[34]

attitudes to the tension between rich and poor, see Balch, "Rich and Poor."

31. John's Gospel speaks of disciples being cast out of the synagogue (John 9:22, 34–35; 12:42; 16:2).

32. *t. Hullin* 2:20, cited by Neyrey, "Loss of Wealth," 146.

33. This scenario is presented as a likely possibility by Neyrey, "Loss of Wealth."

34. The long story in John 9 about a blind man Jesus healed exemplifies the initial

Disciples, then, may be ostracized by their families; the process may well reflect also on the honor of the families. Such marginalization is likely to lead to economic poverty, hunger, verbal abuse, and other forms of persecution. Jesus foreshadows these elements of exclusion and reviling by naming them in the "beatitudes" (Matt 5:11–12; Luke 6:22–23). Mark 13:12 (= Matt 10:21) also anticipates family conflict, leading even to the death of disciples:

> Brother will deliver up brother to death, and the father his child,
> and children will rise against parents and have them put to death.

Jesus himself, rejected by his home community, narrowly escapes death (Luke 4:16–30). Despite Jesus' warnings, there is little evidence in the Gospels, apart from the incidents mentioned above, of active persecution of Christian disciples by their families. Neither Jesus nor his followers are thrown out by their families—they leave voluntarily[35]—yet there is abundant evidence in the New Testament of opposition to Christians and to their message. A few examples: Acts 7 reports the stoning of the deacon Stephen for his testimony to Jesus; Acts 28:22 witnesses to the widespread disrepute accorded to the Christian "sect" in Rome; 1 Peter is concerned for a Christian response to verbal abuse (1 Pet 3:16; 4:4, 14). In today's world also, there are many cultures in which becoming a Christian is regarded as disgracing the family heritage, and potential disciples, facing threats of rejection, expulsion, and bodily harm, must balance the cost of allegiance to family over against allegiance to Jesus.

Loss of Status

Jesus' call to self-denial and discipleship is a difficult one. In his close-knit society, one's honor is symbolized by family and by wealth, so that to give up reliance on these things is to detach oneself from the social matrix in which one has standing. It may then be difficult, if not impossible, to maintain one's social status.[36] A decision to follow him involves radical deviation

---

stages of such treatment: the man's response to Jesus generates conflict with his parents.

35. Downing, "'Honor' Among Exegetes," 72.

36. "Status" is a multidimensional composite of power, prestige, wealth, education, ritual purity, family, and ethnic group position, etc., according to Meeks ("Social Level of Pauline Christians," 201). The "social level" of the early Christians has been the subject of considerable debate. Earlier scholars assumed that Christianity was a movement of the lower classes. However, a new consensus has emerged, acknowledging the heterogeneous

from the norms of society, and this evokes strong negative reactions—the consequences are shameful. But for Jesus, the symbols of worldly honor are nothing in comparison with the honor of participating in the kingdom of God. The new communities of Christians, strongly distinctive from the dominant society and often radically opposed to its values, faced shame and persecution as cohesive minority groups. But in these communities, mutual support and sharing compensated for the loss of natural family and material resources (Acts 2:42–47).

THE MOTIVATIONS FOR SELF-DENIAL

The Gospels point to some factors that provide motivation for self-denial. Some have been mentioned above, and all are related in a foundational way to honor.[37] First we'll consider two prepositions (*heneken* and *dia*) that occur in Jesus' sayings, and then see how some "avoidance and attainment goals" are suggested in the texts.

The Prepositions *Heneken* and *Dia*

Jesus' disciples are called to lose their lives "for my sake and the gospel's" (Mark 8:35). These words point to a reason for the disciples' willingness to deny themselves and to lose their lives.[38] English translations for the preposition *heneken* include "on account of," "because of," and "for the sake of." These could convey a range of nuances, from simple causation to

---

nature of the communities, especially in urban centers (Holmberg, *Sociology and the New Testament*, 21–76). We must be careful not to generalize the Christian communities—the social context of Jesus' Aramaic, largely rural movement is not the same as that of the church in Jerusalem, nor of the Pauline Asian communities of a later period (Holmberg, *Sociology and the New Testament*, 39).

37. The forms of motivation discussed here may not be the only ones in operation. For example, the truth-claims of Jesus may, for certain people, prove so compelling that they motivate discipleship, yet in Jesus' ministry such claims are often upheld by the provision of miraculous signs, a powerful attestation of his divine status, and therefore a representation of honor. In the case of the "Good Samaritan," self-denial is motivated by compassion; although this story is a dynamic illustration of humility and service, it is not a call to discipleship in the same sense as the "self-denial" sayings we have been dealing with here.

38. Koch ("Self-Denial," 838) says that the expression "for my sake and the gospel's" points to "the definitive mark of self-denial, for it embodies the fundamental motivation which underlies all true self-denial."

a suggestion of purpose. The preposition *dia* is often interchangeable with *heneken*, and both may express motivation, though not necessarily so.

Heneken and *dia* are often used in the Gospels to indicate a reason for the persecution of Jesus' followers; this usage reveals no motivation for self-denial, for the persecuted are in fact passive in this situation.[39] This persecution "on account of Jesus" is based on the disciples' association with him, who is already in disrepute, and on their words uttered and actions done in his name[40]—the disciples share the dishonor of the master.

In other places, though, these prepositions *do* give some indication of motivations for self-denial. In such cases the translation "out of consideration for" often seems appropriate, where the consideration may refer to something either in the past or in the future. Self-denial may be a movement that has its basis in prior facts; for example, I may be willing to lay down my life because Jesus has called me to be a disciple. On the other hand, self-denial may be propelled by a future orientation; for example, I may be willing to lay down my life in order to obtain desirable consequences to come, or because of the fear of undesirable consequences if I don't.

Motivation Based on Knowledge of Jesus

In the "saving/losing" saying, disciples are asked to lose their lives "for Jesus' sake" (Mark 8:35; Matt 16:25; 10:39; Luke 9:24). Similarly, Jesus expects that disciples will leave homes and kindred "for my sake" (Mark 10:29) and "for the sake of my name" (Matt 19:29). What is it about Jesus and his "name" that provides sufficient reason for this kind of renunciation of everything? Certainly, the possibilities of persecution and loss of life do not function as inducements. A motivation to follow Jesus must be substantial enough to outweigh these negative consequences. The texts don't give details about the basis of motivation, but they do insist that such self-denial is founded on a fundamental loyalty to Jesus. For those who become attached to him, the person and way of Jesus is so compelling that all other considerations fade.

39. The ill-treatment of disciples is "because of me" (Mark 13:9; Matt 5:11; 10:18), "on account of the Son of Man" (Luke 6:22), "because of my name" (Luke 21:12, 17; Matt 10:22; 24:9; Mark 13:13; John 15:21), "for the sake of righteousness" (Matt 5:10), and "on account of the word" (Mark 4:17).

40. Ps 44:22 expresses the same idea, and is quoted in Rom 8:36, "for your sake we are being killed all day long."

The person of Christ lies at the very root of Christian self-denial. Only on the basis of a personal commitment that supersedes all others can self-denial be contemplated and sustained. Commitment and loyalty to a leader are, of course, functions of the honor in which he is held. His "name" symbolizes this honor, and the honor of the disciples is bound up in the honor of Jesus and the reputation of his name. In each of the Synoptic Gospels, the narrative that precedes the "saving/losing" saying has presented Jesus as one who, by his words of authority and deeds of power, has shown himself worthy of the honor of his followers. He has also reciprocated this esteem to his followers, by calling them, feeding them, teaching them, shepherding them, commissioning them, and making them privileged participants in his mission.

This process is illustrated in the early chapters of Luke's Gospel. These chapters function as a demonstration of the high honor in which Jesus' name is held. Looking for clues to explain why Peter, James, and John "left everything and followed Jesus" (Luke 5:11), we find that Luke has provided evidence of Jesus' honorable birth and childhood (Luke 1, 2), his baptism, replete with divine attestation of Sonship (3:22), his complete genealogy right back to "Adam, son of God" (3:23–38), his successful rebuttal of an honor challenge by the devil (4:1–14), his public claim to divine status as an anointed prophet—a claim that is contested but vindicated (4:16–30)—powerful exorcisms, with the demons testifying to his divine status (4:31–37, 41), miraculous healings (4:38–40), a statement of Jesus' divine mission (4:43), and a miracle involving his supernatural knowledge about fish (5:1–10). All this functions as a defense of the "name" of Jesus. The fishermen are convinced, and on account of Jesus they leave everything and follow him.

Motivation Based on Consideration of the Gospel and the Kingdom

A motivation that is future-oriented is also discernible in these sayings—an awareness of the "not yet" element of the kingdom of God. In Mark we find "for my sake and the gospel's" (Mark 8:35; 10:29), and Luke's version of the latter verse substitutes "for the sake of the kingdom of God" (Luke 18:29). These references to the gospel and the kingdom of God reveal a motivation that, while in no way detracting from commitment to the person of Jesus, yet looks beyond his earthly ministry to the wider spread of his message (cf.

Mark 13:10) and the growth of the rule of God.[41] The disciples, according to Mark 6:7–13, have already been involved in these enterprises, and it seems likely that their investment in the gospel and the kingdom are strong motivations for the casting aside of purely personal interests. Compared with the maintenance of societal norms, the larger purpose of God is a "higher legitimating norm."[42]

A similar motivation is given in Matt 19:12, concerning those who "make themselves eunuchs for the sake of the kingdom of heaven." This rather shocking form of radical self-denial probably refers to disciples who have chosen to remain single and celibate, thereby transcending family ties, in order to facilitate their ongoing participation in kingdom work.[43] A life that is "thoroughly shaped by God's reign" is "consequently lived in its service and at the same time directed towards it."[44]

Avoidance and Attainment Goals

Motivation may be expressed in terms of avoidance and attainment goals, that is, one may say *no* to oneself in order either to avoid something negative or to achieve something positive, or both.[45] How are these forms of motivation expressed in the Gospels, especially in regard to self-denial?

Avoidance Goals

Shame is used as a motivating consideration in many sayings and parables of Jesus. For example, being "cast into outer darkness, with weeping and gnashing of teeth" is no doubt intended to discourage laziness and unfaithfulness in servants. In the eschatological parables, shame functions as negative motivation (e.g., Matt 22:11–14; 24:45–51; 25:14–30 and parallels). Forgiveness and deeds of mercy are motivated by references to prison,

---

41. Cf. Acts 28:20, where Paul is in chains "for the sake of the hope of Israel." Also 1 Cor 9:23, "I do it all for the sake of the gospel, so that I may share in its blessings."

42. May, "Leaving and Receiving," 145.

43. Wolff ("Humility and Self-Denial," 153) believes the words refer figuratively to Jesus and to John the Baptist, but see the extended discussion in Barton, *Discipleship and Family Ties*, 191–204.

44. Wolff, "Humility and Self-Denial," 153.

45. Malina, "Pain, Power and Personhood," 162–64.

torture, curses, and eternal fire, symbols that evoke situations of shame (Matt 18:32–34; 25:31–46).

Similarly, the avoidance of shame is a significant factor in the setting of the self-denial sayings. What is to be avoided is not social shame in this world, for it is made abundantly clear that discipleship involves persecution and many losses, the shame of which must be endured. The shame to be avoided (as in the examples above) is ultimate divine disapproval, that is, eschatological shame. So the Son of Man "will be ashamed" of those who have been "ashamed of Jesus" (Mark 8:38; Luke 9:26); in other words, failure to attach oneself to Jesus in this life will mean being disowned by him when he comes in glory.

Matthew uses the language of "denial before the Father in heaven" to express the same predicament: ultimate public dishonor for those who will not say *yes* to Jesus (Matt 10:33; Luke 12:9). This recalls the possibility of exclusion from the kingdom referred to by Jesus in other contexts (e.g., Matt 7:23; 25:10–13; Luke 13:27; 14:24). Matthew sees the *eschaton* in terms of judgment by God, who will "repay everyone according to deeds done" (Matt 16:27); the shame of a negative judgment is a strong motivation here to act upon the self-denial sayings (Matt 16:24–26). Likewise, in Matt 10:15 the judgment for the "unworthy" is likened to the shameful end of Sodom and Gomorrah; readers are left to deduce the fate of those "unworthy" who do not take up the cross and follow Jesus (Matt 10:38).

The eschatological shame of those who may "gain the whole world" yet "lose their life" is clearly proclaimed in the "saving/losing" sayings. In Luke 17:32–33 this ultimate disgrace, the loss of life, is illustrated by the example of Lot's wife; the message of this passage, anticipating the sudden coming of "the days of the Son of Man," is urgent: deny self and avoid shame!

Attainment Goals

A number of positive motivations appear in the Gospels. Invariably, these can be regarded in terms of honor. Honor, it is universally agreed, is a value worth pursuing. Jesus recognizes that the rich, and those who promote themselves and parade their piety, already have the reward they seek (Matt 6:2, 5, 16; Luke 6:24); this reward is contrasted with that which God will provide (Matt 6:6, 18). Eschatological honor awaits those who love enemies: their reward will be great, and they will be called sons of the Most High (Luke 6:35; Matt 5:45); and those who keep the commandments will be called great in the kingdom of heaven (Matt 5:19). Similarly, those who are willing to deny themselves, take up the cross, and follow Jesus are promised eschatological rewards. I have grouped these in four categories.

(A) APPROVAL

Jesus has a positive estimation of faithful followers who confess him in the world, and he will recommend them to the Father, who will himself honor them (Matt 10:32, 37–38; Luke 12:8; John 12:26).[46]

(B) HONORABLE STATUS

Those who humble themselves, "leave all," and accept low status for Jesus' sake are promised positions of high honor in the kingdom to come. Jesus presents his disciples with images of themselves enjoying the exalted status of judges and privileged guests (Matt 19:27–28; 23:12; Mark 10:31; Luke 9:48; 22:30).

(C) INHERITANCE AND REWARD

Those who have renounced family and riches, and are persecuted for their faith, are promised divine vindication and will inherit eternal life and treasure in heaven (Matt 5:3, 10, 12; 19:29; Mark 10:21; Luke 6:20, 23).

(D) SALVATION

Those who are willing to "lose their lives" and endure suffering for Jesus' sake are promised the transcendent quality of life which is "eternal" (Matt 10:22; 19:29; Mark 8:35; John 12:25). Salvation is sometimes described as "entrance into the kingdom of God" (Mark 10:17–25) or "into the joy of the Lord" (Matt 25:21, 23). The language of these promises was not new to Jesus' disciples and the earliest Christians, for the blessings of the age to come were the common expectation of the people of Israel. However, Jesus claims in these texts that he is the one through whom the reception of the

---

46. Malina, "Patron and Client," 11–18, identifies Jesus as "a broker of the kingdom of Heaven, offering to put people in contact with the heavenly Patron" who, in turn, will provide for them. See also Neyrey, *Honor and Shame*, 42–44.

promises will come. In Jesus' distinctive restoration eschatology, "Israel's hopes are redefined and remolded around him and his own agenda for the kingdom."[47] By appropriating the promises for those who will commit themselves in total allegiance to him, he provides a strong motivation for them to endure and transcend whatever negative consequences will result from their radical discipleship.

The earliest Christian preaching follows the same motivational pattern as that of Jesus, giving as warrants the exalted stature and power of the risen Jesus (e.g., Acts 2:32–36; 3:13–16), the "attainment goals" of honor and blessing from God (Acts 2:38–40; 3:19–20, 25–26), and the avoidance of eschatological shame (Acts 2:21, 40; 3:23).

In terms of Maslow's well-known motivation theory, it is evident that the motivations discussed above appeal to the higher levels of his "hierarchy of needs."[48] Jesus' emphasis on self-denial in fact relativizes *all* levels of need. Jesus does not deny these needs, but urges his disciples to look to God for their satisfaction. The Father will take care of physiological needs and needs for safety and economic security, just as he does for the birds and flowers (Matt 6:19–34), and the need for social relationships is to be filled by the new family of Jesus-followers (Mark 3:35; 10:30). The needs for esteem (honor) and for what Maslow calls "self-actualization"—possibly equivalent to John's expression "abundant life" (John 10:10) or Paul's term for maturity (*eis andra teleion*, Eph 4:13)—are those that, for Jesus, are best met by God alone. By placing the bestowal of divine honor, salvation, and eternal life before his disciples, Jesus promises the satisfaction of the deepest and highest human needs, providing a powerful motivation for turning aside from self-gratification in this world.

Finally, it may be objected that self-denial for the reward of eschatological honor is still self-seeking. Not so, for Jesus never condemns the seeking of honor in itself; rather, he clarifies from whom it is to be sought. Honor granted by God is the honor most to be desired. Therefore, Jesus drastically relativizes the seeking of honor on any other basis than allegiance to himself and to the Father. The following comment by Rudolf Bultmann relates the idea of reward to the quest (perhaps subconscious) for personal authenticity—the subjective honor in which one knows one's own true worth:

---

47. Wright, *Jesus and the Victory*, 338.

48. Maslow, *Motivation and Personality*.

The motive of reward is only a primitive expression for the idea that in what a man does, his own real being is at stake—that self which he not already is, but is to become. To achieve that self is the legitimate motive of his ethical dealing and of his true obedience, in which he becomes aware of the paradoxical truth that in order to arrive at himself he must surrender to the demand of God—or, in other words, that in such surrender he wins himself.[49]

THE LEGITIMATION OF SELF-DENIAL

Several other passages from the teachings of Jesus promote the attitude of self-denial by providing an alternative view of honor, shame, and family. In addition, they affirm those who have denied themselves on Jesus' account.

As we have seen, it was Jesus' expectation that those who would deny themselves and follow him would experience negative social consequences. Because "self" in their culture was largely socially determined, self-denial was also largely a social phenomenon. For the disciples, commitment to the radical new Way of Jesus the Messiah required reevaluation of their previous loyalties and renunciation of the control of social conventions over their lives. To step out of the race for honor was to invite the negative judgment of shame from those still engaged in competing. This loss of honor might include hostility, ridicule, slander, and persecution. It could result in alienation from family and other groups, and possibly the loss of livelihood.

The earliest Christians often really did find themselves in difficult social positions. They were certainly regarded as (what sociologists now term) "deviant," i.e., as departing radically from the social norms. They were variously seen by Jews and Romans as separatists and fanatics, labelled as outsiders and troublemakers, and persecuted as such. How do groups respond in such situations? Philip Richter has examined modern typologies of "destigmatization techniques" employed by those whom society has labelled as deviants.[50] In applying this typology to the New Testament writings of Luke and Paul, he finds that neither writer favors acquiescence to this kind of labelling, or entertains the possibility of capitulation to societal norms, but that both use a variety of techniques to deal with stigmatization. One of these, used by both writers, is the strategy of redefinition, in which

---

49. Bultmann, *Theology of the NT*, 1:15.

50. Richter, "Social-Scientific Criticism," 266–309.

the stigma of being a "Christian" is reinterpreted as a badge of honor.[51] For Paul, for example, the cross is salvation (1 Cor 1:18), and loss is gain (Phil 3:8); in the Gospels, the least is the greatest (Luke 9:48), and the last is really first (Luke 13:30).

Although many of the antithetical sayings examined above use the future tense, expressing the certainty of eschatological reversal, some use the present (e.g., Luke 9:48) and may be considered to be examples of "redefinition of the situation" by Jesus. How one sees things depends on the point of view taken; Jesus encourages his followers to have regard to the higher court of reputation, "for that which is highly-esteemed among people is detestable in the sight of God" (Luke 16:15b).

In Jesus' social context, his use of redefinition can be seen as a prophetic strategy, the purpose of which is to expose common attitudes and practices as inconsistent with the kingdom of God. For example, Jesus redefines certain kinds of public piety as hypocrisy (Matt 6:2). But a converse use of redefinition is evident as well, as in Jesus' reinterpretation of the "least" as the "greatest" (Luke 9:48); by this means Jesus reveals the high esteem of his lowly hearers in the sight of God, opening them to a new view of things and motivating them toward discipleship. The Beatitudes can be seen as examples of this, as I will show below.

In the context of the early church, redefinition also became a strategy for encouraging followers of Jesus to persevere in their social difficulties of loss and persecution. For example, the Letter to the Hebrews often redefines shame as honor.[52] But the Gospels themselves function in this way. By taking account of Matthew's and Luke's editorial activity, the texts that are commonly called the Beatitudes may legitimately be viewed as material that assisted its first-century readers to reassess their social situation in terms of honor and shame.

---

51. Those hostile to Christianity, of course, used the technique in reverse: Pliny the Younger wrote of the Christians' courage as "obstinacy" in his Letter to Trajan, 10:96, in Ferguson, *Backgrounds of Early Christianity*, 557–58.

52. DeSilva, *Hope of Glory*, 144–77; also, deSilva, "Despising Shame" and *Bearing Christ's Reproach*. In Heb 12:8 suffering is reinterpreted as the honor of being disciplined as a child of God.

The Beatitudes as a Redefinition of Shame

Matthew's Gospel presents Jesus' Beatitudes (Matt 5:3–12) as part of a compilation of Jesus' teachings, probably given many times to different audiences. Luke reproduces only four of these (Luke 6:20–23) along with . corresponding woes (6:24–26). It has been suggested that these beatitudes function as statements that "destigmatize" followers of Jesus.[53] Jesus addresses these statements to those who are in unhappy situations in this world. Each statement contrasts the present situation with a future one. For example, "Blessed are the poor in spirit, for theirs is the kingdom of heaven." Perhaps it is more accurate to say that the contrast is between how we (or the world) view ourselves and our situations and how God views us and our situations. Many of the statements can be construed in terms of honor and shame.[54] Jesus may in fact be predicting unhappy situations awaiting those who follow him and "take up his cross"—that is, situations of persecution (explicit in Matt 5:11–12 and Luke 6:22–23) and ascriptions of dishonor (that is, shame) resulting from transformed beliefs of Christians and a clash of values that leads to changed behavior. But Jesus insists that in each of these states or situations his followers are "blessed."

This expression of "blessing" has a strong background in the Old Testament. For example, "Blessed is the one who does not walk in the counsel of the wicked" (Ps 1:1). Though the English word "blessed" implies a blessing bestowed by another (for example, God), this implication is not necessarily present in the original languages (Hebrew *ashrei* and Greek *makarios*), where the word is an adjective describing a happy state. It has been variously translated as "happy" and "fortunate," but another suggested translation is "honorable."[55] If we accept this translation, Jesus is saying something like, "How honorable (in God's eyes) are those whom the world does not honor." Jesus expects his followers to act contrary to cultural expectations (as he himself did) and consequently to lose public esteem. However, Jesus "revalues what has been disvalued, and honors what has been shamed."[56] Jesus has reinterpreted his followers' shame (according to the dominant society) as honor (according to himself and to God). He has affirmed their

---

53. Richter, "Social-Scientific Criticism."

54. White, "Grid and Group."

55. Hanson, "How Honorable!" Similarly, the words for "woe" (Greek *ouai* and Hebrew *hoi*) should be translated "how shameful" or "shame on. . ."

56. Neyrey, *Honor and Shame*, 167.

identity as part of the new kingdom of God. Their righteousness, hidden from their persecutors, is valued by God. On this basis, therefore, those who have suffered the consequences of radical self-denial for the sake of Jesus are motivated to persevere in the midst of social conflict. This, then, is another method by which Jesus encourages faithful following, including self-denial and all that entails.

The Redefinition of Family

By setting human honor and shame against the ultimate honor and shame which comes from God, Jesus provided a new perspective which not only enabled his followers to deny themselves, but also enabled them to cope with whatever social consequences might result from their decision to be disciples. However, this redefinition went only part way toward the fulfilment of Jesus' purposes.

He was bringing to light a new manifestation of the kingdom of God, a people whose identity was continuous with, but distinct from, the traditional Israel. Sociologically, however, Jesus' disciples must live their lives in the midst of a dominant society that viewed the new distinctives as deviant, and which therefore tended to treat the disciples with contempt and hostility. Identity and social wellbeing were so embedded in family solidarity that isolation or exclusion on account of deviancy would be devastating. In such a culture, a "self" cannot exist alone. Where could disciples look for human support? Divine honor may compensate for the loss of societal honor, but is there a compensation for the loss of one's family? The Gospels say *yes*. In several passages Jesus enigmatically but effectively redefines "family."

Mark 3:31–35 (with Matt 12:46–50 and Luke 8:19–21) tells how Jesus' mother and brothers are standing outside, waiting for Jesus, who is inside, surrounded by a crowd as he teaches. When told about his family, some of whom may have been involved in accusations against him (Mark 3:21), Jesus asks, "Who is my mother and my brothers?" Then to the crowd he says, "Here are my mother and my brothers; whoever does the will of God is my brother and sister and mother." We see here that Jesus intends his followers to adopt and display the kinds of relationships that are analogous to natural kinship. This would be a new society whose members would "do the will of God." It was "a new social world in the making."[57]

57. Barton, *Discipleship and Family Ties*, 82. These relationships are often described as those of "fictive kin"—a sociological term for a group that supplies pseudo-familial

Mark 10:29–30 (with Matt 19:28–29 and Luke 18:29–30) reinforces this perspective. Jesus anticipates the provision of fictive kin relationships in place of the natural familial relationships that have been "left" for the sake of Jesus and the gospel:

> There is no-one who has left house or brothers or sisters or mother or father or children or fields, for my sake and for the sake of the gospel, who will not receive a hundredfold now in this age—houses, brothers and sisters and mothers and children, and fields, with persecutions—and, in the age to come, eternal life. (Mark 10:29–30)

The relationships that have been "left" include brothers, sisters, mother, father, and children. The relationships "received" include all of these except father; this absence is significant, for the new "family" would acknowledge only God as Father—all patriarchal structures would be abolished. The preeminence of the new "family" over the old is represented symbolically by the "hundred-fold." It is very clear that this is no eschatological promise, but that the new "family" would have real existence in the present evil world ("now in this age") and would certainly include persecutions.[58]

The groups that formed around Jesus (both the itinerant band that traveled with him and the groups centered on the homes of his friends) may be regarded as prototypes of the new inclusive "family" we see coming into existence in the book of Acts, after the coming of the Holy Spirit. Paul makes much use of the metaphor of the family—the church is "the household of God" and its members are brothers and sisters—but the metaphor had its origin in Jesus' teachings, as the above passages illustrate. Disciples who had "denied themselves" and experienced consequent social shame are empowered by Jesus' affirmation of them as part of the renewed eschatological family who are the true children of God and heirs of his kingdom.

Jesus' Teaching on Self-Control

We have considered the Beatitudes, but much of the other ethical teaching of the Sermon on the Mount touches on aspects of self-denial, for Jesus

support. Hellerman's *Ancient Church as Family* highlights the many ways in which the community of early Christ-followers was self-consciously a family.

58. Matthew's version refrains from specifying a present-age fulfillment, focusing more on the *eschaton*, with places of honor for the twelve disciples who will judge Israel (Matt 19:28). Neither Matthew nor Luke includes the reference to persecutions.

teaches God-centeredness rather than self-centeredness. Many of his sayings here reflect his emphasis on relinquishment of worldly honor, as in Matt 6:1–6, where he contrasts ostentatious prayer behavior that seeks human affirmation with humble prayer that is rewarded by God. But other sayings seem simply to require self-control.

Temptations to sexual sin are universal, but Jesus insists that we must say *no* to bodily appetites, like lust, in which we are so easily ensnared (Matt 5:27–30). The hyperbolic language he uses (tearing out the eye, cutting off the hand) emphasizes the seriousness of this kind of self-mastery.

Similarly, Jesus' "do not be anxious" passages address our natural human tendency to be overly concerned with the provision of our basic needs (Matt 6:25–34; Luke 12:22–31). Jesus, using "how much more" arguments, invites us not to deny the needs, but to relinquish the anxiety and worry that too often accompany them; again, our focus is to be on God, not ourselves.

Jesus' instruction to "turn the other cheek" (Matt 5:39) appears counter-intuitive. It calls us to attend to our natural instincts for self-defense, retaliation, and revenge, and urges us to put them to one side (say *no* to them). It encourages us to control the anger and frustration that arise when we are challenged, and to work against the impulse to retaliate. This is not to say we must be "doormats." We are to respond by taking action that is motivated by love, not by a desire to pay back. Jesus did this: when he was mocked, he did not retaliate (Mark 14:65; 15:16–20; cf. Isa 50:6; 1 Pet 2:21–23).

In John's Gospel, Jesus presents a discourse centered around the extended metaphor of the vine that bears fruit (John 15:1–11). This imagery, with a rich background in the Hebrew Scriptures, is the controlling motif in this passage. Believers are to be rooted in the person of Christ, rather than in the heritage of Israel, but what is the fruit? The most common sense of the "fruit-bearing" metaphor is moral (in the Gospels, Paul, Hebrews, James, and Jude). The context here suggests love (15:9), joy (16:20, 22, 24), and peace (16:33). Jesus says that only by "abiding in the vine" can lasting fruit come; he is the source. The implication is that his followers must say *no* to their own efforts at self-promotion, acquisition of virtues, self-advancement, self-actualization, and such. Yet Jesus' imperative—that believers are to "remain" in him—amounts to a call to attend continually to faithful perseverance, avoiding the distraction of things that may lead one off-track and cause (in terms of the vine metaphor) unfruitfulness, withering, and eventual destruction (15:6). It is an implicit call to self-control and self-discipline.

SUMMARY: WHAT DO THE GOSPELS SAY ABOUT SELF-DENIAL?

We've seen that the self-denial of which Jesus spoke can be described as an individual's rejection of the sources of honor that are traditional, normal, and foundational in human society, out of consideration for a higher source of honor—the honor granted and promised by God. Our reading of a wider range of texts in the Gospels sought nuances in Jesus' teaching relating to honor and the self, and we've seen that this material strongly supports this understanding of self-denial. We can now summarize this in a different way.

Self-Denial Is Humility and Service

To deny oneself is to refuse to give oneself honor. It is the renunciation of an orientation toward the self, and the abandonment of a quest for status. Jesus castigates self-exaltation, and legitimates the humbling of oneself by affirming humility and service as attitudes and actions greatly valued by God. Self-denial is thus fostered and empowered by the knowledge that one is now honored by God and that this honor will be manifested publicly in the future. One's relationship with the gracious Father relativizes all other relationships of honor.

Self-Denial Requires Disattachment

Regarding the possible social consequences of self-denial, the Gospels indicate that Jesus' relativization of family and wealth is so strong that disattachment from them can be considered not merely a consequence of discipleship, but actually a prerequisite. Both family and wealth exert strong claims, and both are sources and symbols of honor. However, a person's adherence to them is seen as a hindrance to following Jesus. Self-denial, as the denial of family, is founded upon the benevolence of the divine Father; as the denial of possessions, it is enabled by the reality of heavenly riches;

as the denial of status in society, it is founded on the higher honor of Jesus, the one to whom primary loyalty is due.

Self-Denial Is Purposeful

Our examination of motivations showed that self-denial is founded upon the honorable reputation of Jesus and upon participation in the kingdom of God; it is motivated negatively by the prospect of divine disapproval (eschatological shame) and positively by the prospect of divine honor (eschatological rewards).

Self-Denial Is Honorable

Finally, we have seen that aspects of self-denial and its consequences are reinterpreted in the Gospels, particularly in Jesus' Beatitudes. Self-denial is motivated and affirmed by Jesus' new perspective in which aspects of discipleship that are not honored by the dominant society are honored by God, and in which the new eschatological family of God becomes a reality.

Self-denial, then, is a radical renunciation of one's own claims on life, wealth, and worldly honor. It amounts to a revaluation of one's temporal life, one's goals and priorities. It involves a relativization or decentering[59] of one's self, as a holistic response of attachment to Jesus, to whom his followers owe loyalty and honor. It is "self-abandoned adherence to the giver of life."[60] The "self" is not obliterated or lost, but is reoriented, as exemplified by Jesus' own submission to God: "Not what I want, but what you want" (Mark 14:36).

JESUS AS A MODEL OF SELF-DENIAL

Before examining the rest of the New Testament, we should note some aspects of Jesus' example as a practitioner of self-denial. Jesus demonstrated in his own life what he expected of his followers. The temptation narratives

59. For the term "decentering" I acknowledge Volf, *Exclusion and Embrace*, 69–71, who draws attention to Paul's similar but more explicit formulation of self-denial as crucifixion: "I have been crucified with Christ, and it is no longer I who live. . . . The life I now live in the flesh I live by faith in the Son of God who loved me and gave himself for me" (Gal 2:19–20). We will reflect on this in the next chapter.

60. Rensberger, "Asceticism," 145.

(Matt 4:1–11) depict Jesus effectively saying *no* to Satan's offer of power and authority ("All these kingdoms will be yours") and to the possibility of satisfying his own forty-day hunger ("Tell these stones to become bread"). His life was characterized by humility and service to others. We have already noted that he took the role of a servant in washing his disciples' feet (John 13:1–17). Though Jesus was tired and thirsty, he put his own needs aside and focused on the needs of the woman he met at the well (John 4). He was a wandering preacher, traveling, contrary to the usual practice of a teacher, in order to proclaim the kingdom and to minister. Consequently, he was often homeless, and had "nowhere to lay his head" (Luke 9:58). He modelled appropriate responses to lack of money and possessions, teaching his disciples to pray for their daily bread. He abstained from taking a wife, dedicating himself totally to the service of God to which he had been called. His attitude is well summed-up in his statement, "I seek to do not my own will but the will of him who sent me" (John 5:30; 6:38) and in his prayer in the garden of Gethsemane, "not my will, but yours be done" (Luke 22:42). For Jesus, self-denial entailed risking his own honor, enduring the shame of rejection, and, ultimately, laying down his life for the honor of his friends (John 15:13), an action motivated and energized by the mutual honor and love that flowed between him and his Father. Jesus is, in fact, the ultimate model of self-denial: he does not "save his life" at the cross (Mark 15:31) but loses it for the sake of others (Mark 10:45).

Imitation of Jesus

Only in John's Gospel do we find words of Jesus that explicitly urge his followers to imitate him. After washing his disciples' feet, Jesus says, "You also ought to wash one another's feet, for I have set you an example, that you also should do as I have done to you" (John 13:14, 15). John identifies the motivation for this action as love: "Having loved his own who were in the world, he loved them to the end" (13:1). This is a significant motivation for self-denial that doesn't receive much attention in the Synoptic Gospels, but John emphasizes it, and it is prominent also in the letters of John, as we will see.

Jesus' extended metaphor of the shepherd and the sheep (John 10:1–18, 26–28) illuminates the nature of discipleship. The shepherd leads and the sheep follow after him. He promises to reward the faithful following (read self-denial) of his "sheep" with eternal life (10:27–28). However, the cross casts its shadow in this image, for the shepherd (Jesus) of his own accord "lays down his life for the sheep" (10:11, 15, 17, 18). Jesus' motivation is love: "No one has greater love than this, to lay down one's life for one's friends" (15:13).[61] This is what Miroslav Volf calls "self-donation"—the self-giving love that is at the very center of the New Testament, not just the Gospels.[62] It can be considered the ultimate expression of self-denial. Jesus explicitly identifies this love as the model for his followers to imitate: "Love one another, as I have loved you" (15:12). In fact, this imperative is a "commandment" (13:34; 15:12), because love is to be the distinguishing mark of his disciples (15:35), the characteristic that will be the strongest witness to the unbelieving world.

61. In John 13:37–38 Jesus questions Peter about his avowed intention to "lay down his life" for Jesus. We find, later in the story, that he is not able to do it; instead, he denies Jesus.

62. Volf, *Exclusion and Embrace*, 24–25.

CHAPTER 3

Self-Denial in the Pauline Letters

If the idea of "denying oneself" holds a significant place in Jesus' teaching, we can perhaps expect that it would be reflected somehow in early Christian writings apart from the Gospels. I am convinced that the idea of "denying oneself"' does indeed appear many times in the rest of the New Testament. The New Testament writers were themselves followers of Jesus, and they appropriated what he had taught them. In their writings the concept of self-denial is echoed, reaffirmed, developed, and demonstrated.

The New Testament vision of what is entailed in "denying oneself" becomes wider and deeper when the writings of Paul and the personal witness of his life are considered. Paul gives a strong emphasis on the subjugation of personal interests for the sake of Christ and the gospel. I believe this is linked to and founded on Paul's appropriation of divine honor, implicit in the acceptance of the new identity given "in Christ." Moreover, Paul's life demonstrates a personal application of these principles: he renounces the esteem he had as a Pharisee, and effectively "takes up the cross daily" as a disciple and imitator of Jesus, convinced that all his losses are more than compensated for by the incomprehensible depth and breadth of the love of God that has been lavished on him.

Paul hardly ever quotes Jesus, but sometimes seems to echo his teaching. Paul's language is not the same as Jesus' language, because his social context was different, as was his calling, his role, and his audiences.[1] However, I find that Paul's writings are fully consistent with what the Gospels report with regard to Jesus' self-denial sayings. There is significant continuity

---

1. See further Wright, *Paul*, ch. 8.

between Jesus and Paul, in both teaching and practice.[2] I will treat Paul's writings in the order in which we find them in the Bible, although this is not the order in which they were written. Because I am interested in tracing this theme through the whole of the New Testament, I will include the letters that some scholars consider to be "deutero-Pauline" or "pseudo-Pauline" and will treat them all as having been written by Paul or under his direction.

ROMANS

The "Old Self" and the "New Self"

In explaining the gospel of Christ and its significance and implications for followers of Jesus, Paul refers to "our old self," which was crucified with Christ (Rom 6:6). In what sense does Paul use this expression, and how does it relate to self-denial? The word translated "self" is *anthrōpos*, the word for a human person, or, in other contexts, for humanity as a whole. But he is not talking about one's individual human nature here. In the context of the soteriology that Paul is expounding in this letter, he is drawing attention to the fact that the death of Christ has made a difference to the way in which Christians should think of themselves. Though he uses the word "old" only once, the passage proclaims that the cross, and the baptism by which Christians identify with Christ's death and resurrection, marks a dividing line between the "old" and the "new." It is not that our sinful nature has been destroyed by crucifixion, because we are obviously still sinful people. Rather, it speaks of transformation from the old quality of life (enslaved to sin and death) to the new quality of life (freed from that bondage so that we can live a godly life). In the previous chapter Paul has drawn the old/new distinction in terms of two dominions, those of Adam and Christ (Rom 5:17). As a collective expression, "our old self" is the state of our humanity before we grasped the gospel and responded in faith. It was characterized, indeed dominated, by ignorance of God, rebellion against God, and sin generally. But for those who have embraced faith in Christ, "our old self" is obsolete.[3] What has been destroyed is "the body of sin"—not, of

---

2. I will avoid speculation about the trajectory of transmission of Jesus tradition that Paul received. This topic is well covered by others, e.g., Dunn, *Jesus, Paul, and the Gospels*; Schoberg, *Perspectives of Jesus*.

3. Jewett, *Romans*, 402–3.

course, our physical body, but the extent to which our existence has been attached to the sinfulness of the world and determined by it. This "old self" has been put out of action—"rendered powerless" (NIV)—by identification with Jesus on the cross.[4]

This is a legal reality, but the experience of it is to be realized by every believer. Verse 11 clarifies this: we must *consider ourselves* to be dead to sin, but alive to God in Christ Jesus (6:11). Paul is obviously not speaking about destruction of a person's total self. While there is life there is "self," but what changes is the way we think about ourselves—the perspective with which we view ourselves. John Stott offers a helpful analogy:[5] I should think of my former life, before I put my faith in Christ, as Volume I. My life as a Christian is Volume II. Of course, some aspects of my life have continuity in both "volumes"—such things as personality type, strengths and weaknesses, family, skills, history, and place—but it is not appropriate for me to live as if I were still in Volume I. This way of thinking of two selves helps me to have a little more clarity about what self-denial means. It means, at the very least, that we must say *no* to things that were characteristic of the "old self" but have no legitimate place in the "new self." We must not let ourselves be controlled by the powers that Christ has conquered.

Denying the "Old Self"

In Rom 7:5–13 Paul writes about the written Law of God. Because he is now both a Jew and a follower of Christ, he is concerned to elucidate a Christian interpretation of the Law. His main point is to insist that there is nothing wrong with the Law. In making this point, he identifies the real culprit: the sin that lies within us, stirring up our desires and inciting us to disobey. He explains this in detail by giving us a window into his personal experience— the inner tensions that are involved in the everyday application of the "two selves" perspective that he introduced in chapter 6.

Scholars still debate whether the "I" in Rom 7 refers to Paul's experience before conversion or after it, or whether he uses "I" in a representative way. It seems to me that Paul is talking about himself and his struggle to understand his own behavior.[6] J. I. Packer notes that Paul is not describing a struggle with sin, as if he is trying to decide whether or not to sin, because

---

4. Dunn, *Romans 1–8*, 318–20.

5. Stott, *Men Made New*, 45.

6. I find that I am in agreement with Packer, "'Wretched Man' Revisited," 70–81.

he is walking in "newness of life" (6:4). Rather, he is recognizing that "the flesh," which is his former self, refuses to lie down and die. Robin Griffith-Jones makes the same point:

> [Paul's "I"] can now specify where the good and the evil lie; it can spot the conflict between mind and deed and so come to understand its own will. The self sees its own mind in action healed: here it is, analyzing, assessing, and deciding. Intellect and will are no longer blocking the subject's knowledge of God. There is no delusion here, as there was at 6:1 and 6:15; just an incapacity. The mind is learning a new lesson: the lesson of its own limitation.[7]

Paul is expressing what everyone knows: that there's a difference between what we ought to do and what we actually do. We want to do what is right, but despite our knowing that Christ has conquered the power of sin, and although we reckon ourselves dead to it, the remnants of sin are still present, threatening to bring us down and take over our lives. This is the aspect of "self" that it is appropriate to deny—to say *no* to taking the backward step into the attitudes and behaviors that we once engaged in. Charles Cranfield writes, "It is the new self that I recognize as my true self and with which I desire to be more and more fully identified. This new self I do not have to deny; for it is the Holy Spirit's work in me."[8]

A New Identity as Children of God

In Rom 8:12–14 Paul continues to contrast death and life. Death is due to sin, and life is to be found in Christ, as he has explained in the previous chapters, but now we learn that it is only by the Holy Spirit that we can obtain life and peace (8:5–6). It's the same kind of life-death antithesis as we have seen in Jesus' "finding/losing" saying in Mark 8:35—love your life and lose it, lose your life and find it. Paul is a little more graphic: we must actively "put to death" our old way of living in order to live by the Spirit rather than "according to the flesh" (8:12–13), that is, by human standards. Here Paul is viewing "the deeds of the body" as the way of living he elsewhere labels *sarkikos*, "fleshly" (1 Cor 3:3; 2 Cor 1:12). This way of living is not conformed to the ways of the Spirit of God. It is earthly, and is characterized by human inclinations—jealousy, strife, and insincerity. Paul's argument in

---

7. Griffith-Jones, "'Keep Up Your Transformation,'" 154–55.
8. Cranfield, "Self-Denial," 145.

this passage is based on the new relationship by which Christ-followers can legitimately call God "Father," using even the more intimate term "Abba." Who are we, then? We have a new identity as God's children (8:14–17). Consequently, we will want to say *no* to our old ways of living and begin to live in the new way.

There are two other connections with Jesus' "self-denial" saying, in which he tells his followers to "take up the cross" (Mark 8:34). Paul insists here that children of God must suffer with Christ before they can be glorified with him (8:17). In place of the language of "following" as the essence of discipleship, Paul often uses the word "walk" (*peripateō*) to designate a way of life.[9] This is a conventional metaphor that has its origin in Hebrew.[10] Jesus (and here, the Spirit) sets the direction in which we should walk (8:4).

Transformation and Renewal

On the basis of all that he has written so far to the Roman Christians, in Rom 12 Paul appeals to them to think deeply about themselves and to make a response. He assumes that his readers have the ability to think reflexively—to give close attention to the "self," to examine their own lives, attitudes, values, and allegiances—and to be persuaded to seek transformation.[11] Paul wants them to present their bodies as "a living sacrifice" to God (12:1). By "body" (*sōma*) he means not just the physical flesh, but the whole person. He gives the reason for this total submission to God: it is their *logikē latreia*. Scholars still seek for a definitive translation of these words. Whether it is "reasonable service" (KJV), "true and proper worship" (NIV), "spiritual worship" (NRSV), or "truly human vocation,"[12] Paul is convinced that there is a fundamental necessity for followers of Christ to offer the totality of their selves to the God who has been so merciful and gracious to them.

Paul goes on to explain in more practical terms what this submission entails. There are two imperatives: "Do not be conformed to this world, but be transformed" (12:2). Negatively, this is not so much a renunciation of the world as a refusal to shape one's life according to the patterns set

---

9. E.g., Rom 6:4; 8:4; 13:13; 14:15; 1 Cor 3:3; 7:17: 2 Cor 4:2; 5:1; 10:2, 3; Gal 5:16 and others.

10. Hebrew *halak*, e.g., Ps 1:1.

11. Paul similarly urges self-examination (individually and corporately) in 1 Cor 11:28 and 2 Cor 13:5.

12. Dürr, "Your Fully Human Vocation."

by human culture. Positively, there is a *metamorphōsis* to be made, and it must be done by "the renewing of your minds." They should "re-envision their own identity by the sustained engagement of their imagination on a typological reworking of their own selves."[13] This reworking implies self-denial in the sense that the old ways of thinking about oneself are replaced by fresh ways, and consequently habits are reshaped. Using the analogy of a computer, we might say that it's like gradually becoming familiar with a new operating system. This personal transformation by the renewal of the mind has a purpose: the discernment of "what is good and acceptable and perfect" (12:2), that is, the standards of thinking and living that are in line with God's will. In other words, transformed and renewed believers cannot legitimately rely on worldly standards to decide for themselves what is good to think about or what is the right way to live.

In verse 3 Paul reflects further: "I say to everyone among you not to think of yourself more highly than you ought to think"—one's position or honorable status must be seen in relation to God, who gives the grace that is the only reliable basis for self-evaluation. Paul plays on the word for "think" (*phronein*) here, beginning with *hyperphonein*, which in the context means to think oneself to be superior, but ends the sentence with *sōphronein*, which means to be sober-minded, showing proper moderation and good judgment. These words would be associated in the minds of the Roman readers with the cardinal virtue *sōphrosynē*, a broad term that signified a sound mind characterized by self-control, moderation, and a deep awareness of one's true self.[14]

An important aspect of this "sober thinking" is the recognition of one's own roles and gifts (*charismata*), "each according to the measure of faith that God has assigned." Paul mentions many such gifts in verses 4–8, and seems to imply that, as people are differentiated with individual personalities and motivations, sound discernment will lead a person to think, for example, "I am a leader, but not a prophet" or "My gift is compassion, but I am not a leader." Another aspect of "sober thinking" is the realization that one must speak and act for the benefit of the whole community of believers—"We, who are many, are one body in Christ" (12:5). Here Paul is undermining the Roman system of status and honor.[15] The kinds

13. Griffith-Jones, "'Keep Up Your Transformation,'" 138.

14. Thorsteinsson, *Roman Christianity*, 94. These qualities are also reflected in Jewish intertestamental literature, e.g., Sir 18:19–33.

15. Oakes, *Reading Romans in Pompeii*, 98–126.

of self-promotion and competition for honor that were so prevalent in Roman society (and often in ours) are inappropriate for Christians, for there is equal honor for all believers—honor that is given by God. Indeed, Paul counsels his readers to "outdo one another in showing honor" (12:10).

This is an aspect of the demonstration of love. In a passage reminiscent of 1 Cor 13, Paul explains some of the characteristics of love by using twelve participles (not commands) in verses 9–13. He goes on to say that this attitude of love and attention to others must be extended to outsiders, even to enemies. He gives special emphasis to the avoidance of revenge—followers of Jesus must deny themselves the luxury of paying back evil for evil (12:17–21). This means that they will often have to say *no* to some insistent natural inclinations when they are faced with hostility.

New Clothing for the "New Self"

In Rom 13:11–14 Paul writes further on the subject of saying *no*: "Let us lay aside the works of darkness and put on the armor of light." The motivation is eschatological: "the day is near." Here the clothing image refers to ethical behavior, and the darkness and light refer to the old way of life and the new, as in 1 Thess 5:5–8. Six examples of bad behavior are given in v. 13, and then we read a surprising expression in v. 14: "Put on the Lord Jesus Christ." The clothing metaphor, which Paul has also used in Gal 3:27, has been described as "a powerful expression of early Christian mysticism."[16] It probably means that we are to "become one with him and to be fully encompassed in his likeness and identity."[17] This being so, gratification of the "desires of the flesh" is incompatible with "living honorably" (13:13–14). It is probable that Paul has in mind not only the desires that lead to the unethical behaviors he has mentioned here, but also the desires that lead to the pursuit of social dominance, prestige, and honor, as we have seen in Rom 12.[18]

16. Jewett, *Romans*, 827.

17. Porter, *Letter to the Romans*, 256.

18. Jewett, *Romans*, 828.

Self-Denial of the "Strong" for the Interests of the "Weak"

Romans 14 and 15 relate to specific practical concerns in the New Testament churches, but they contain important principles that relate to the ways in which Paul wants Christian believers to think of themselves; they therefore relate to self-denial. Paul writes,

> We do not live to ourselves, and we do not die to ourselves; if we live, we live to the Lord, and if we die, we die to the Lord; so then, whether we live or whether we die, we are the Lord's. (Rom 14:7–8)

The Greek can be more literally translated as "No one of us lives or dies in relation to himself or herself." Paul wants his readers to recognize that they must view all things in relation to God, and to deny egocentricity. Brendan Byrne summarizes this by saying that "the whole of Christian existence, including death, takes place within the sphere of Christ's lordship and under his authority."[19] This basic theological and ethical principle is the foundation on which all decisions about everyday matters are to be based. The issues in the context of this passage have to do with whether people abstain from eating certain foods, and whether people treat one day of the week as more special than another. Both practices involve self-denial of a sort, and Paul maintains that if they are done "in honor of the Lord" all is well. However, the stronger message is that there must be no passing of judgment between those who do and those who don't. Paul, viewing himself as one who is "strong" and who is free to eat anything and treat all days alike, insists that there must be no despising of the "weak," for God is the only judge who matters. Instead, "walking in love" (14:15) means managing one's behavior so that it puts no "stumbling-block or hindrance in the way of another" (14:13). This is the attitude that places limits on one's conduct for the benefit of others. When our behavior affects other people (and surely this is the case most of the time) we need to consider their needs as more important than our own. Failure to do this, Paul writes, may lead to God's work (the nurture of others, the growth and reputation of the church, etc.) being destroyed (14:20).

Paul now moves on to speak of the obligation of his readers to do more than merely avoid giving offence by using their freedom. "We who are strong ought to put up with the failings of the weak" (15:1)—referring to those who are not as well informed about God's grace. This points to an attitude beyond mere tolerance, for the verb *bastazein* more usually means

19. Byrne, *Romans*, 413.

to carry, in the sense in which Paul uses it in Gal 6:2, "bear one another's burdens." In the Greco-Roman culture, the weak were supposed to submit to the strong, but Paul counsels otherwise, confirming the perspective of Jesus, as we saw in the humbling/exalting saying and the first/last sayings. To lend a hand to a neighbor in this way is to behave altruistically rather than egoistically. Speaking to "each of us" including himself, Paul says that we must not "please ourselves" (15:2). "Pleasing oneself" seems to be equivalent to "living in relation to oneself" (14:7). In Gal 1:10 and 1 Thess 2:4 Paul writes that he does not try to please people by a show of rhetoric or by preaching a truncated gospel; this would be the kind of people-pleasing that is self-serving, seeking worldly honor. But there is an obligation to "please our neighbor for the good purpose of building up the neighbor." The goal is the mutual edification of believers (14:19) and the peace and harmony of the Christian community (15:5). This is a reversal of the cultural expectation that we should build up our own group by disparaging other groups. Paul grounds this selfless attitude in the example of Jesus: "Christ did not please himself" (15:3). Something from Isa 53 might well have been quoted at this point, but Paul chooses Ps 69:9. Paul has quoted it without changing the words, but in the psalm "you" is God and "me" is the author, whereas Paul probably intends a reapplication, such that "you" is the Christian community and "me" is Christ. In other words, the shameful insults directed at Jesus-followers fall on Jesus himself: he bears their shame, he is in solidarity with the powerless ones; he does not please himself, but bears the burdens of others.

1 CORINTHIANS

We Do Not Belong to Ourselves

In 1 Cor 6:19 and 20 Paul writes to the Corinthians regarding fornication: it is a sin against the body, and is to be shunned. He sums up his exhortation with the statement, "You are not your own, for you were bought with a price, therefore glorify God in your body." It is as natural for us as for the Corinthians to consider ourselves as autonomous individuals who have the right to do what we like with our bodies. We presume that we have ownership of ourselves. But Paul here forces us to reckon with the redemption that Christ accomplished by giving his life on our behalf. This redemption (1:30) was a purchase, as Paul specifies in 7:23, using the analogy of the slave market, where slaves became the property of the person who bought them. Followers of Christ now belong to him, not to themselves (3:23), because he has paid for them with his own blood, as Paul is reported to have said in Acts 20:28. "God now has the title deed to their bodies."[20] It is therefore appropriate for Christians to deny any presumption of rights to autonomy and self-determination where such rights conflict with or disregard God's claim of ownership.

Self-Denial for the Sake of the Other

First Corinthians 7 deals with Paul's answer to a question asked by the Corinthians about marriage.[21] Scholars disagree about the interpretation of some aspects of Paul's answer, but what is clear to all is that Paul strongly affirms the exclusivity of the marriage bond between a husband and a wife. He states this position in 7:2–5. Within this passage he writes that "the wife does not have authority over her own body, but the husband does; likewise, the husband does not have authority over his own body, but the wife does" (7:4). That is, in the context of sexual relations within marriage, each partner yields their body to the other. This is a practical example of what Paul says elsewhere: "Let each of you look not to your own interests, but to the interests of others" (Phil 2:4). Within marriage, then, Paul advocates self-denial, in the sense of control of one's sexual urges, for the sake of the other.

Self-Denial in Marriage and Singleness

The larger issue, though, is whether Paul is advocating a more general level of ascetic self-denial by promoting the value of singleness as opposed to marriage. Verse 1, taken as Paul's own position[22] (rather than as a quotation of a communication from the Corinthians), states both his advocacy

---

20. Garland, *1 Corinthians*, 239.

21. The background to the issues of 1 Cor 7 are ably set out by Danylak, *Redeeming Singleness*.

22. This is the traditional interpretation, reflected in the KJV and NASB translations. Most newer translations view the statement "It is good for a man not to touch a woman" as a quotation from a letter written by the Corinthians. However, Danylak (*Redeeming Singleness*, 173–211) argues convincingly that it is unlikely that the Corinthians would have written the sentence, since there is very little evidence of ascetic mentality in Corinth at the time.

of sexual abstinence and hence his preference for singleness: "It is good for a man not to touch a woman" (where "touch" is a euphemism for sexual relations). For him, this preference is a "particular gift from God" (7:7, 8). However, though he consistently condemns all forms of *porneia* (sexual activity outside of marriage), which was rampant in Corinthian society, he avoids imposing his preference for singleness on others—he does not want to "put any restraint" on them (v. 35). On the contrary, he encourages marriage: "Each man should have his own wife and each woman her own husband" (7:2); "it is better to marry than to be aflame with passion" (v. 9); "if you marry, you do not sin" (v. 28); "let them marry; it is no sin" (v. 36); "she is free to marry" (v. 39). Despite this recognition of the value of marriage, Paul argues that to refrain from marriage is better (v. 38). His two reasons, given in 7:28 and 32–34, are that a married person will experience "distress in this life" and that an unmarried person can be more single-mindedly engaged in "the affairs of the Lord" and how to "please the Lord." Thus, his overall opinion is that singleness is preferable but not required. However, he counsels both the married and unmarried to "remain as they are"—neither to seek marriage nor to deny it. It is notable that, for both groups, self-control is essential. Paul acknowledges the possibility of lack of self-control (*akrasia*, v. 5) in marriage, and the necessity for the unmarried to exercise self-control (*enkrateuomai*, v. 9).

A second issue related to self-denial is Paul's advice in 7:29–31. When he writes, "Let those who have wives be as though they had none," is he implying that men should lead a celibate life even if they are married? There are four more similar phrases that could indicate that Paul is advocating ascetic practices. However, the reasons he gives require us to understand that he is appealing here for his readers to consider their whole lives in an eschatological framework: because "the appointed time has grown short" (v. 29a) and "the present form of this world is passing away" (v. 31b), everyday relationships and activities need to be relativized. Although marriage and business are legitimate realities, they are not "ultimately determinative as to how one lives as a 'Christ person' in the world."[23]

Relinquishing Freedom

First Corinthians 8 is a short chapter that begins to answer a question raised by the Corinthians: is it OK for Christ's people to eat food that has

23. Fee, *First Epistle to the Corinthians*, 377.

been offered to pagan idols? Paul offers the same principles here as he does in Rom 14. He will say more in chapter 10 of this letter. He first reassures the Corinthians that there is nothing inherently wrong about eating such meat, and they should be free to eat it: "We are no worse off if we do not eat, and no better off if we do" (8:8). However, some believers have a "weak conscience" and will not eat such meat, considering it to be defiled (8:7). If they see other believers exercising their freedom to eat, those with a "weak conscience" may be tempted to betray their conscience and sin. Exercising the freedom to eat has become a "stumbling-block" (8:9) that may cause a Christian to fall back into idolatry and thus be "destroyed" (8:11). Therefore, the loving thing to do in such a case is to avoid insisting on one's rights, to say *no* to flaunting one's freedom in certain matters, and to be ready to relinquish it altogether for the sake of others' wellbeing.

Relinquishing Rights for the Sake of the Gospel

First Corinthians 9 is Paul's extended defense of his apostleship. In this chapter he outlines his right to earn his living by working for the spread of the gospel. He is entitled to some material support, and he backs up his claim with Scripture: an ox is not to be muzzled while threshing. Nevertheless, he writes, he did not use this right (12, 15, 18). He has said *no* to his entitlement. In order to win more people to Christ, Paul has practiced self-denial—he has chosen not to enjoy some benefits that he is actually entitled to. In fact, he has chosen to become a "slave" (19)—to take up voluntarily the position of one who has very few rights. He is not a slave to human authorities, but to God, who has commissioned him with a task. In striving to fulfill this task of proclaiming the good news of Jesus to all, he relinquishes the trappings of the identity he is most comfortable with, because he wants to identify more closely with those he wants to "win."

> To the Jews I became as a Jew, in order to win Jews. To those under the law I became as one under the law (though I myself am not under the law) so that I might win those under the law. To those outside the law I became as one outside the law (though I am not free from God's law but am under Christ's law) so that I might win those outside the law. To the weak I became weak, so that I might win the weak. I have become all things to all people, so that I might by any means save some. I do it all for the sake of the gospel, so that I may share in its blessings. (1 Cor 9:20–23)

Notice that the phrase "for the sake of the gospel" is the same as that spoken by Jesus as part of his classic self-denial saying: "Those who lose their life for my sake, and for the sake of the gospel, will save it" (Mark 8:35).[24]

Running the Race: Athletic Self-Discipline

Paul follows this explanation of his behavior with an extended metaphor: if you're running in a race, there's a prize at the end that's worth aiming at, and so, in order to win it, you have to exercise some discipline and self-control (*enkrateia*).

> Do you not know that in a race the runners all compete, but only one receives the prize? Run in such a way that you may win it. Athletes exercise self-control in all things; they do it to receive a perishable garland, but we an imperishable one. (1 Cor 9:24–25)

Paul calls the Christian community to copy him in running the race, which is an exercise of often-uncomfortable self-denial. Again, the motivation is an eschatological one: he looks forward to obtaining what Peter calls "the crown of glory that never fades away" (1 Pet 5:4). Paul adds here a comment about his behavior that sounds like ascetic self-punishment:

> So I do not run aimlessly, nor do I box as though beating the air, but I punish my body and enslave it, so that after proclaiming to others I myself should not be disqualified. (1 Cor 9:26–27)

Gordon Fee correctly points out that Paul is here using athletic metaphors, which must not be interpreted literally.[25] He is talking about exercising *enkrateia*—mastery over oneself in all things (v. 25). His "body" (*sōma*) stands for his whole person, as it does in Rom 12:1. "I enslave my body" (v. 27) repeats what he has written in verse 19: "I have made myself a slave." In other words, Paul has voluntarily accepted certain limitations and curtailments of his freedom, and probably also some of the hardships commonly experienced by slaves, so that his ministry is more effective. It is therefore inappropriate to see here an example of self-flagellation, as if physical self-punishment could help to further spiritual progress.

---

24. Paul uses the expression *dia to euangelion*, while Mark uses *heneken tou euangeliou*. The two prepositions are often used interchangeably.

25. Fee, *First Epistle to the Corinthians*, 484–85.

Relinquishing Self-Centeredness

First Corinthians 10:23–33 addresses the same concern that Paul writes about in the second half of Rom 14, and especially 15:1–3. Here, as in Romans, his point is that, for the building up of the Christian community, believers should relinquish self-centeredness and instead focus on what is beneficial for others. The passage is framed by two statements about "seeking one's own advantage." "*Do not seek your own advantage*, but that of the other" (10:24). "I try to please everyone in everything I do, *not seeking my own advantage*, but that of many, so that they may be saved" (10:33). The context is what seems to have been an everyday problem for the Corinthians: whether or not to eat meat that had been sacrificed to idols. This is one of the areas in which the Corinthians appear to have had a "me first" attitude. But Paul is concerned that, whatever is decided, the primary consideration should be the effect on the other person. It is not that Paul expected Christians to give up their own interests altogether, but love must be the controlling factor, motivating a temporary giving up of one's freedom if that freedom would cause problems for a neighbor or friend (cf. 1 Cor 9:19). Thus, Paul would deny himself a meat dinner if eating it would offend someone else present at the meal. Paul tries to "please everyone" (10:33) not in the sense of a flatterer, in order to gain approval for himself, but in the sense of his rendering service to Christ. "As Christ's slave, he also renders service to others regardless of the cost to himself."[26]

Self-Denial Motivated by Love

Paul's famous description of Christian love for others (*agapē*) is found in 1 Cor 13. This chapter is important in the context of Paul's teaching about the management of worship meetings. His point is crystallized in 14:1—"Pursue love and strive for the spiritual gifts," but in arguing for the primacy of love he gives two examples of great personal sacrifice (13:3). First, "If I give away all my possessions. . ." The word for "possessions" is the word *huparchonta*, used by Jesus: "None of you can become my disciple if you do not give up all your possessions" (Luke 14:33). Paul insists that even such radical renunciation is worthless if the motivation is not love. The second example is less specific: "and if I give over my body to hardship so

---

26. Garland, *1 Corinthians*, 502.

that I may boast" (NIV).[27] He may be referring to the kinds of deprivations and suffering that he lists in his second letter to the Corinthians (2 Cor 11:21–30)—he "boasts" of these things that demonstrate his weakness in the service of the gospel, and for which he expects an eschatological reward (Rom 5:2–3).[28] But again, if he suffers these things without being moved by an attitude of love, he is "nothing." Literally, Paul writes, "It profits me nothing" (*ouden ōpheloumai*), which reminds us of the words of Jesus, "What will it profit them (*ōphelei*) to gain the whole world and forfeit their life?" (Mark 8:36). Self-denial (personal sacrifice or "losing one's life" for the sake of others) is here motivated by love.

The chapter characterizes love in many ways, and at least two of these relate to self-denial. Paul writes that love is not arrogant (13:4). The word *phusioō* means to be conceited or "puffed up." Paul has noted previously that "knowledge puffs up, but love builds up" (8:1). The purpose of much of this letter is to bring correction to people who are, sadly, "puffed up" with their own importance (4:6, 18; 5:2). In contrast to this attitude, "love does not insist on its own way" (13:5). An alternative translation is: "Love is not preoccupied with the interests of the self."[29] In fact, *agapē* "excludes a range of types of emotion and behavior that are all based in the individual I-perspective."[30] The other kinds of "love" are different: *eros* always seeks its own interests (to be satisfied with or to possess the object of love, to gratify its desires), and *philia* denotes devotion to one's own, whether self or family, chosen friend or lover. But *agapē* "stands in opposition to all that can be called 'self-love.'"[31]

---

27. Some versions (e.g., ESV, NASB, KJV) follow the Greek texts that have "burned" (*kauthēsomai* instead of *kauchēsomai*). There are several weighty reasons for rejecting this reading; see Metzger, *Textual Commentary*.

28. "Boasting" is something Paul mentions often in his letters. It is not to be taken in the sense of self-exaltation, for it usually has the sense of giving glory to God, as in Jer 9:23–24, which Paul quotes in 1 Cor 1:31.

29. Thiselton, *First Epistle to the Corinthians*, 1026.

30. Engberg-Pedersen, "Radical Altruism," 205.

31. Thiselton, *First Epistle to the Corinthians*, 1050. We must note, though, that there is a legitimate kind of self-love that honors the self as a valued creation of God, and hence must not be denied.

2 CORINTHIANS

Paul the Humble Apostle

Paul's second letter to the Corinthians deals largely with his relationship to the Corinthian believers. He has a divine mission as an apostle, but because of difficulties in Corinth he finds it necessary to explain himself to them, hence he writes of his conception of his own identity—he reveals how he thinks of himself. Paul has a clear self-awareness as an authoritative apostle who has been sent by God to serve God's people (2:17). He is confident in fulfilling his calling to this ministry, but he is always eager to maintain that this confidence is not in himself but comes from God. "Such is the confidence that we have through Christ toward God. Not that we are competent of ourselves to claim anything as coming from us; our competence is from God, who has made us competent to be ministers" (3:4–5). This statement answers the question he asked in 2:16, "Who is sufficient (competent) for these things?" His task requires resources that he knows do not naturally lie within him, and so he relies on God. He has a mature and realistic self-understanding that is characterized by humility. He says that he is "nothing" because God is the source of all that he does.[32] How, then, should we understand his many references to "boasting"?

Paul's Boasting

Paul insists that he does not proclaim himself; rather, he proclaims Jesus Christ as Lord and views himself as a slave (*doulos*) serving the Corinthian fellowship (4:5) and as a servant (*diakonos*) of God (6:4). Nevertheless, he does not shrink from "commending himself" (4:2; 6:4). In one sense, self-commendation can be seen as self-exaltation, and Paul strongly denounces this practice. He writes in 3:1 and 5:12 that he does not need to commend himself by providing letters of recommendation, and he disapproves of those who exalt themselves by comparison with others (10:12). His principle regarding self-commendation is given in 10:18—"It is not those who commend themselves that are approved (*dokimos*), but those whom the Lord commends." Paul echoes here what Jesus has said plainly in the Gospels: "Those who exalt themselves will be humbled" (Matt 23:12). In other words, it is ultimately useless to seek the approval of other people—to want

---

32. Barnett, *Second Epistle*, 579.

to have one's ego stroked by the endorsements of others. Self-denial means saying *no* to this. Paul values God's approval more than any honors that the world may want to give him. Therefore, when we read that Paul "commends himself" (4:2; 6:4) it is not self-exaltation. He is not seeking the approval of the Corinthians, because he knows that God approves his work and commends him. What he has accomplished is only the result of God's grace in his life (4:1).[33] It is the "open proclamation of the truth" (4:2) of the good news that speaks for him, and his faithfulness to his calling (1:12; 6:4–10) proves his sincerity.

Similarly, when we notice that Paul refers to "boasting" twenty times in this letter, it is necessary to make a distinction between "boasting in the Lord" (10:17) and boasting "according to human standards" (*kata sarka*, 11:18). In his culture, self-promotion, political rivalry, and personal pride were taken for granted as normal elements of Roman citizenship,[34] but Paul boasts of the things that show his weakness (11:30; 12:5, 9). In contrast to those who "boast in outward appearance and not in the heart" (5:12), and those whom he calls "false apostles" (11:13), whose boasts lack authority and are merely self-exalting, Paul lowers himself in order to elevate those he cares for (11:7). His boasting is not focused on himself: elsewhere he boasts only that *others* have been faithful (Phil 2:16; 1 Thess 2:19; 2 Thess 1:4).

Paul's Alternative Worldview

Paul can do these things because of the power of God in his life—"a reality that radically transforms the significance of his circumstances."[35] He offers a vivid testimony in 2 Cor 6:4–13, a passage replete with the language of honor and dishonor. He characterizes his ministry as "servant of God" (6:4) by a long list of items, supplementing the examples of suffering he has already mentioned in 1:4–11 and 4:8–9. He has shown "great endurance" (v. 4) in experiencing difficulties caused by hostile people and uncomfortable circumstances (vv. 4–5). He has been able to do this by engaging the virtues

33. See Hafemann, "Self-Commendation," 66–88.

34. Witherington, *Shared Christian Life*, 40. See especially Plutarch's *On Praising Oneself Inoffensively*, in which he presents cases for and against boasting. For recent studies see Wojciechowski, "Paul and Plutarch on Boasting"; Smit, "Paul, Plutarch"; and Pawlak, "Consistency."

35. Hafemann, *2 Corinthians*, 271.

and graces and empowering he has received from God (vv. 6–7). These are not his natural attributes or self-generated moral qualities, or the results of positive thinking.[36] In an impressive collection of evocative verbal oppositions (vv. 8–10), he lists the ways in which the world views him and treats him (in dishonor), and the ways in which he might perceive himself (as poor, sorrowing, even dying). He contrasts these with the convictions of his new alternative worldview: he is honored, he is true, he is known by God, always rejoicing, truly rich, really living. This attitude depends on his having made choices about which worldview to adopt and inhabit. He has chosen to turn away from certain modes of thinking and responding that might be regarded as natural to humans. To this extent he has denied himself. He exhibits here the mind-set that he enjoins in Rom 12:2—"Do not be conformed to this world, but be transformed by the renewal of your mind." He has been forced to rethink everything, with Christ at the center.

The "Outward Self" and the "Eschatological Self"

In order for us to "deny ourselves" we need to have a realistic perception of who we actually are. Paul helps us here in this letter, which is rich in theological anthropology. Many of Paul's disclosures of his own self-perception, based on his transformed theocentric worldview, have a broader application to the ways in which his readers should think of themselves. One passage that is a good example of this is 2 Cor 4:16–18. In these verses Paul writes "we" as he does throughout the letter in reference to himself and Timothy, but here this "we" must include his readers, as it often does in other passages. He makes a statement that could almost be merely a common-sense observation: "Even though our outer nature (*anthrōpos*) is wasting away, our inner [nature] is being renewed day by day." The following verses make it clear that he is not just saying that, although we are getting old and frail, we are still learning. Nor is he making a Greek dualistic distinction between the physical body and the immortal soul. Rather, in the context of what he calls "slight momentary affliction" he is encouraging his readers not to "lose heart" (4:1, 16) by reminding them of the incomparable glory that awaits faithful Jesus-followers. His distinction between the "outer" and the "inner" is eschatological anthropology. The "outer"—the person as a visible being in this world—is "wasting away" because it is transient. The "inner"—the person as a "new creation" in Christ (5:17)—is "being renewed day by day"

36. Hafemann, *2 Corinthians*, 270.

by the Holy Spirit. It is the *esō anthrōpos* (the inner person) that delights in God's law (Rom 7:22). It is unseen but eternal and glorious in the life to come.

Paul demonstrates, then, that the way we think of ourselves depends on our perspective. He recognizes an earthly self and a heavenly self. They are both real, and the existence of neither must be denied. The earthly self is a "tent" but the heavenly self is an everlasting house designed by God (5:1).[37] At present we are "at home in the body" but we look forward to the time when we will be "at home with the Lord" (5:6–9).

No Longer Living for Ourselves

Paul finds it unthinkable that Christ's followers should "live for themselves" (2 Cor 5:14–15). Rather, motivated by the compelling love of Christ, it is right that they should henceforth live "for him who died and was raised for them." Mark Seifrid comments, "Christ died in order to deliver human beings from their fatal bondage to themselves. It is this deadly narcissism of the Corinthians that Paul deals with throughout the letter."[38] Paul's ministry has many aspects, but none of them is done for himself: they are all done for God and for his people (5:13).[39] He has said *no* to promoting himself or seeking fame, because his consideration of the self-sacrificing love of Jesus restrains him from doing so. The self is no longer his center of reference; Christ is now his focus and controlling force. Thus, Paul can say in verse 16, "From now on, therefore, we regard no one from a human point of view (*kata sarka*)." That is, we see all human beings with new eyes, because Christ's love brings a radically new understanding of others.[40] In fact, we see ourselves with new eyes, as recreated people freed from our self-seeking nature and our own constructions of reality. The old has passed away, and everything has become new (5:17).

---

37. Paul's dualism here is theological, not philosophical in the sense of Plato's. "The idea of the body as a tent is different from Philo's and Plato's idea of the body as a prison; a tent is thin, flexible and sheltering" (Lynch, "Transcending Desire," 173).

38. Seifrid, *Second Letter*, 244–45.

39. Barnett, *Second Epistle*, 287.

40. Seifrid, *Second Letter*, 244–46.

GALATIANS

"It Is No Longer I Who Live"

In a striking reference to himself in Gal 2:20, Paul reveals that his identity has been transformed. In fact, he can say, "It is no longer I who live." In the context of the passage, Paul is speaking about dying to the law and living by faith in the Son of God; he obviously intends this to apply to all his readers who have been converted to Christ, and in this sense he is not speaking in an exclusively individualistic way: he uses "I" language to represent the body of believers. But even so, Paul is expressing here what Richard Valantasis calls a "pneumatic subjectivity"[41] in which he repudiates his old self—at least, his old way of thinking—so that he may think and act differently. He no longer lives an independent life of his own.[42] He is a transformed person (cf. 2 Cor 5:17), "a member of a new created order in which life and death are seen from an entirely different perspective."[43] He has renounced his old identity, though it is not a total denial, for he has not lost his human personality, and he remains a Jew. But for Paul "the old order of life is now redundant in light of the new event that had burst upon the world in Jesus."[44] His old identity, in which he saw himself primarily as a Jew, has been transcended by a deeper reality, revealed to him in his meeting Jesus on the road to Damascus. He now sees his identity as primarily determined by being "in Christ." However, the practical outworking of this is not simple, as Paul testifies in Rom 7. Terence Donaldson helps us to understand this:

> [Paul's transformed thinking] has to be understood not as a total abandonment of one set of convictions in favor of another, different and distinct, but as the reconfiguration of one set of convictions around a new and powerful center. In the process, some individual native convictions were abandoned, others radically altered, still others carried over more or less intact, and additional Christian ones introduced.[45]

---

41. Valantasis, "Competing Ascetic Subjectivities," 214–20.

42. Fung, *Epistle to the Galatians*, 124.

43. Mohrlang and Borchert, *Romans and Galatians*, 284.

44. Bird, *Anomalous Jew*, 17–18.

45. Donaldson, *Paul and the Gentiles*, 298.

Overcoming the I-Perspective

In Gal 5 Paul writes again of his freedom from his old way of thinking and being. Christ has set us free (5:1) but we are not to use this freedom to return to bondage. We are not free to do whatever we feel like doing, because that would be self-indulgence—living according to the "flesh" (5:13), which, with its passions and desires, has been crucified with Christ (5:24). Rather, we are free to "become slaves to one another." This expression seems to be an echo of Jesus' saying in Mark 10:43–44, "Whoever wishes to become great among you must be your servant, and whoever wishes to be first among you must be slave of all." Paul explains what he means in 5:16–26, where he contrasts a long list of self-focused attitudes and actions with a set of other-focused virtues, the "fruit of the Spirit," of which the first and greatest is *agapē*. "He overcomes altogether the I-perspective in favor of the shared we-perspective."[46] This is a strong teaching on self-denial. Note especially that self-control (*enkrateia*) is a fruit of the Spirit (5:23). In the context of Paul's argument, it has nothing to do with abstinence, which in itself is not a virtue, but it is a "general stance toward excesses of various kinds,"[47] particularly regarding the ways in which we relate to others. Behaving selfishly is equivalent to what Paul says is "sowing to your own flesh" (6:8), and doing so will reap destruction.

EPHESIANS

A New "Subjective Status"

For reasons that have been well documented by other scholars, I take Paul to be the real author of Ephesians and Colossians, despite some substantial arguments to the contrary.[48] We begin with Eph 1:3–14, where superlatives fail to capture fully the range and abundant goodness of God's bestowal of honor on those who follow Jesus. In Greek, the passage is one long sentence, and the expressions of divine honor pile on top of one another: blessing, adoption, redemption, forgiveness, grace, revelation, inheritance, grace, glory, salvation, and promise.

46. Engberg-Pedersen, "Radical Altruism," 206.

47. Fee, *Galatians*, 223.

48. Fowl (*Ephesians*, 28) gives a comprehensive review of the problems, and concludes that "theologically and interpretively, it does not make much difference whether Paul or a close follower wrote the text."

A typology cited by Wayne Meeks is helpful as another way of describing this bestowal of honor from God. Meeks distinguishes three categories: 1) "objective status," which depends on the structure of one's environment; 2) "accorded status," which is prestige granted by others and exhibited externally; and 3) "subjective status," which is perceived internally and which gives a personal sense of social location.[49] In purely social terms, a disciple of Jesus may suffer losses in all three categories, as we have seen when exploring the Gospels. However, where God is the one who accords status, it is received by faith as a "subjective status," that is, a personal sense of honor and of location, by grace, in the family and kingdom of God. Eph 1:3–14 is a glorious expression of this subjective status, lavishly applied to followers of Jesus. On this strong basis of transformed identity, which he assumes will be accepted and embraced by the Christians in Ephesus, Paul is bold to point out some vivid contrasts with their former way of life, and to highlight some ways of realizing and expressing their new identity.

Denying the "Old Self"

To express the transformation that faith in Christ brings, Paul uses the figurative dichotomy of the "old self" (*palaios anthrōpos*) and the "new self" (*kainos anthrōpos*) in Eph 4:22–24.[50] He speaks of a previous kind of existence, a "former way of life" that was characterized by "trespasses and sins," "passions of the flesh," "desires of flesh and senses," "futility of mind," "darkened understanding," "ignorance and hardness of heart," "insensitivity, licentiousness, greed, and impurity," "corruption, deluded by lusts," "bitterness, anger, wrangling, slander and malice" (2:1–3; 4:17–19, 31). This dismal state was shared by Paul, since he uses "us" in 2:3, though it is doubtful that he participated in every one of these elements. These things are now to be "put away" (*aposthesthai*, 4:22, 25), which can be taken in the sense of "cast off" since the new things are to be "put on" (*endusasthai*, 4:24, "clothe yourselves"). Paul uses a clothing metaphor here, encouraging his readers to put off certain attributes and attitudes and to put on others that are more virtuous.[51]

---

49. Meeks, "Social Level," 202, citing Lipset, "Social Class."

50. See also Rom 6:6 and Col 3:9, 10. The *kainos anthrōpos* in Eph 4:24 is to be distinguished from the *kainos anthrōpos* in Eph 2:15. The latter refers to the union of Jew and Gentile in one "new humanity."

51. Some commentators (e.g., MacDonald, *Colossians and Ephesians*, 304–5) see

The figurative language used here is interesting. The things to be cast off are specified variously, but Paul bundles them up into what he calls the "old self" (*ton palaion anthrōpon*, 22). This expression seems to be a metonymy for the old sphere of existence in which one's attitudes and practices were incompatible with faith in Christ. It is necessary to recognize that the language of "self" here is primarily ethical, not anthropological. That is, it relates to attitudes and behavior rather than to ontology. Nevertheless, the putting off of the "old self" constitutes self-denial to the extent that one's self-perception or identity is defined by the "old self." It would not be too far-fetched to consider that Paul's own relinquishment of at least some elements of his Pharisaical persona is a realization of this principle of putting off the "old self."

To replace the "old self" the "new self" must be put on (24). This "new self" is described as a new creation (cf. 2:10) that is "according to God," having the characteristics of righteousness and holiness (which are characteristics of God) and whatever qualities and virtues are antithetical to the "cast off" things. This is a new self-perception, a reconfiguring of one's way of thinking about oneself, a "renewal of the mind" (23), based on what God has graciously done in Christ. This renewal (*ananeousthai*, present passive, with a continuous sense) is not a one-time act, but an ongoing process by which the Holy Spirit leads us to accept our new identity and live in it. Having said *no* to the old, we need to say *yes* to the new, and this means that it is necessary to dispose of or unlearn old patterns of thinking, feeling, and perceiving, and to learn new ones.[52] Paul fills his letters with guidelines about how to live in this newness of life; the rest of this epistle provides a wealth of such instructions.

---

this "garment imagery" as reflecting, and possibly originating in, the baptismal practice whereby baptismal candidates shed their old clothes and put on new ones following their baptism. This may be the case in Gal 3:27 and Col 2:11–12, where the "putting off" image is used in conjunction with baptism. However, other texts refer to putting on breastplates (1 Thess 5:8), the armor of light (Rom 13:12), and the Lord Jesus Christ (Rom 13:14). Col 3:8–10, as in Ephesians, urges putting off the "old self" and putting on the "new self."

52. Fowl, *Ephesians*, 152.

COLOSSIANS

A Transformed Identity

It is well-known that the letter to the Colossians shares much material with the letter to the Ephesians. I am partial to the not-too-fanciful suggestion that the two letters (together with the letter to Philemon) were written on consecutive afternoons. Thus, much of what I have written about Ephesians can be said also of Colossians. The new "subjective status" of Jesus-followers is expressed a little differently. Christians have been "transferred into the kingdom" of Jesus, from darkness to light (1:12–13); they have been redeemed and forgiven (1:14) and reconciled, so that they are now holy, even "blameless and irreproachable" (1:22), and they are part of his "body" (1:18), "bearing fruit" and "growing in the knowledge of God" (1:10). They are later described as "God's chosen ones, holy and beloved" (3:12). Their identity has been transformed, and they are living now in an "alternative mode of existence."[53] On the basis of this ontological reality their behavior must be consistent.

Resetting the Mind

According to Paul, the human mind in its natural state is dark; it suppresses the knowledge of God (Rom 1:18–32) and is hostile to God (Col 1:21). But in this letter Paul thankfully acknowledges that his readers have "truly comprehended the grace of God" (1:6) and are now able to "be filled with the knowledge of God" (1:9). Their minds have been transformed. However, the transformation is ongoing, as these Christ-followers both allow themselves to be shaped by the Spirit and take active steps to conform their lives to Christ's pattern. As part of his encouragement to them, Paul offers this instruction in Col 3:2: "Set your minds on things that are above, not on things that are on earth." The word for "set your mind" is the imperative *phroneite*, which has the basic meaning "think."[54] Paul assumes that his readers have the capacity to control their thinking—they have choices regarding the content and direction of their thoughts. By "things that are above" Paul seems primarily to mean Christ, who is enthroned in heaven

---

53. This expression is from Valantasis, "Constructions of Power," 800.

54. Rom 8:5–7 expresses the same concept in a different form: setting the mind on the Spirit instead of the flesh.

(3:1), but since he specifies all manner of "earthly things" in the subsequent verses, the "things above" would include the whole range of characteristics of the new life in Christ.[55]

To use a current metaphor, it seems that, for Paul, the natural mind is "programmed" for sin. Perhaps his exhortation to "set your mind" might correspond to pressing the "reset" button, but I think it is better to use the "operating system" analogy that I used earlier—to let our minds be "programmed" not by natural human considerations (the "things of earth") but by the whole new "operating system" of God's Spirit (the "things above"). If we are to follow Paul's urging, we must say *no* to the old system, delete it, and let the new be installed.

Putting On the "New Self"

The clothing metaphor makes a reappearance in Col 3:9–10. As in Ephesians, Paul insists that the old way of life must be put away. If baptism symbolizes "putting off the body of the flesh" (2:11), the new life of the Spirit must entail getting rid of the attributes, attitudes, and values that characterized and expressed the old life, the "old self" (*palaios anthrōpos*, 3:9). Paul gives rather a lot of examples: fornication, impurity, passion, evil desire, greed, idolatry, anger, malice, slander, abusive language, and lies (3:5–9). These old things must be "stripped off" (3:8, 9), even "put to death" (3:5). But it is not just attitudes and practices that are "put to death," for Paul writes "*you* died" (*apethanete* in 2:20 and 3:3). This can be taken merely as a reminder of their baptism, which is a symbol of burial and resurrection in Christ (2:11–13), but I think Paul wants these Christians to embrace this new realization of themselves as "resurrected" people. It is a mind-setting project (3:2) in which the self is to be reimagined. What they were before is no more. They have "taken up their cross" and followed Jesus to the crucifixion of their old identity. So now they must "put on" the new identity, the "new self" (*neos*) that is "being renewed in knowledge according to the image of its creator" (3:10). The old way of life must therefore be rejected because it is inconsistent with the new identity. It is eminently reasonable, then, for committed followers of Jesus to say *no* to their pre-conversion persona—to deny the aspects of the "self" that are incompatible with faith in Jesus. They must now say *yes* to the attitudes, values, and practices that *are* compatible and consistent with faith in Jesus; they must "put on" or "clothe

55. See further Keener, *Mind of the Spirit*.

themselves" (3:10, 12, 14) with a post-conversion persona. Of course, this clothing metaphor is not quite adequate to describe what is going on. Renewal is more than just changing our appearance or our actions—it has to happen on the inside, in the heart. Again there is a list—a virtue list (3:12–14) that contrasts with the vice lists (3:5–9): compassion, kindness, humility, meekness, patience, forgiveness, and above all, love.

Inappropriate Self-Denial

However, all is not well in Colossae, as we learn from Col 2:16–19. Paul warns his readers about dangerous people—false teachers who make use of "philosophy and empty deceit, according to human tradition . . . and not according to Christ" (2:8), and who insist on observance of certain rituals and customs arising from what he describes as "a human way of thinking." Scholars have not been able to identify exactly who these false teachers were, but it is clear that they were attempting to promote various kinds of ascetic practices, two of which have implications for our exploration of self-denial.

The one mentioned first concerns "matters of food and drink" (2:16). The Colossians are being urged by the false teachers to submit to regulations such as "Do not handle, Do not taste, Do not touch" (2:21). While these prohibitions may have arisen from an incipient form of Gnosticism, or a legitimate desire to keep Jewish laws, which require one to say *no* to certain natural desires or to things tainted with evil, Paul resists them on account of their merely human, worldly origin (2:20, 22). Bad theology leads to bad practice. These kinds of self-denial are unnecessary, especially if they are being imposed as obligatory behavior, for Christ has set us free (Gal 5:1).

The other concern is the false teachers' insistence on "self-abasement" (2:18) in the context of other dubious expressions of worship. The word is *tapeinophrosunē*, which is translated as "humility" in 2:23 and 3:12. Humility is an attitude rather than a practice, but it can be expressed in a right spirit, as when one comes submissively before God in prayer. However, here it appears that Paul is referring negatively to a kind of ascetic self-denial—a regimen of fasting or renunciation (perhaps including sexual abstinence) that is intended to promote holiness but is (in Paul's view) merely self-punishment.[56] This word is grouped in 2:23 with "self-imposed piety," which

56. MacDonald, "Citizens of Heaven and Earth," 275. MacDonald notes that early

could refer to religious activities of worldly origin, and "severe treatment of the body," which could cover a multitude of ascetic performances involving physical renunciation and even bodily self-harm.[57] "Worship of angels" in 2:18 may indicate a desire to worship in the same manner as angels, that is, because angels do not eat, drink, or marry, we should copy them.[58]

The false teaching may have been something like this: "Christian baptism is just the first step, and in order to make spiritual progress you must get special advanced wisdom and extra secret knowledge to explore the hidden mysteries and eventually become perfect. To do this you must give up all worldly things, hate the material things, hate even yourself, treat your body harshly, and concentrate on the spiritual things, like angels and visions." This would be ascetic syncretism, mystical piety.

Paul recognizes that these things have "an appearance of wisdom" but he is not in favor of them, because they are merely appearance, and because "they are of no value in checking self-indulgence"—literally, "the gratifying of the flesh" (2:23). "Severe treatment of the body" may, in practice, be little different from Paul's habit of bodily discipline ("I punish my body and enslave it" in 1 Cor 9:27), but the motivation is different. Paul disciplines his body and brings it into subjection to his God-given calling, whereas the ascetics at Colossae seem to be observing a man-made religion, "not holding fast to the head" (2:19), and seeking spiritual experiences that bypass the wisdom and revelation of God. The results are also different: restraining sensual indulgence (the unholy human inclinations and desires) is a major purpose of self-control, and certain kinds of self-denial are appropriate if they help,[59] but the methods referred to here are unhelpful, impotent, and inappropriate.

So it can be seen that Colossians condemns one kind of ascetic self-denial (false humility, severe treatment of the body, submission to decrees that forbid touching and tasting and yet prescribe certain ascetic practices) but advocates another kind—the putting aside of "fleshly" attitudes and

---

church authors use the term specifically to refer to fasting (e.g., Herm. *Vis.* 3.10.6; *Sim.* 5.3.7).

57. This verse is difficult to translate. See MacDonald, *Colossians and Ephesians*, 116–18, for a discussion of alternatives.

58. This interpretation takes "angels" as a subjective genitive. The Jewish notion that angels did not eat, drink, or marry accords well with the transcendent-ascetic philosophy of the Colossian false teachers (Gupta, *Colossians*, 100–101).

59. Compare Paul's approval of celibacy for those who have been gifted with it (1 Cor 7).

actions on the basis of the "alternative mode of existence" in which the Jesus-followers now live. This amounts to world-rejection in a different key from that of the false ascetics. Walter Kaelber suggests the term "inner asceticism"—a discipline that is spiritual rather than physical—that involves "not detachment from or renunciation of any specific worldly pleasure but rather detachment from or renunciation of the world per se. It is reflected in the biblical attitude [John 17:14–16] of being 'in the world, but not of it.'"[60]

The motivation for this discipline of the mind, body, and spirit lies in the indicatives of the first part of the letter, especially 1:12–14 and 2:11–15, which outlines all that God has done for the Colossians in Christ—they are rescued, forgiven, and renewed; therefore (v. 16) they are urged not to return to the power of darkness (1:13). Both letters to the Ephesians and Colossians encourage believers to live a conventional life in households, sustaining the patriarchal structures of society (a strategy of survival in an increasingly hostile environment) with no need for repeated physical, ascetic rituals like those of the Colossian opponents.

PHILIPPIANS

Selfish Ambition: Let It Go

Perhaps Paul's most powerful treatment of matters relating to self-denial is found in Phil 2 and 3. Paul begins his letter with heartfelt prayer for the Philippian believers, and shares some personal reflections about his imprisonment and his hope of meeting them again. His appeal begins in 1:27. Once again his starting point is the gospel of Christ, which is the basis on which his readers are to build their lives. His emphasis here is on the unity of the group. He is talking about their communal life, urging them to "stand firm in one spirit, striving side by side with one mind for the faith of the gospel." In 2:2–4 he explains what this means:

> Be of the same mind, having the same love, being in full accord and of one mind. Do nothing from selfish ambition (*eritheia*) or conceit (*kenodoxia*), but in humility (*tapeinophrosunē*) regard others as better than yourselves. Let each of you look not to your own interests, but to the interests of others. (Phil 2:2–4)

60. Kaelber, "Asceticism," 442.

The word for "selfish ambition" is *eritheia*. It is used five times in Paul's letters.[61] It is the word for acting out of self-interest, contentious rivalry, seeking honor for oneself. NASB translates it simply as "selfishness." In the absence of a single word for self-denial, *eritheia* seems to be the best candidate for the opposite attitude. *Kenodoxia* is similar: literally "empty glory" or conceit, groundless self-esteem. Both words indicate a posture to which Paul says a strong *no*. What he urges instead is *tapeinophrosunē*, humility.

These instructions imply that self-centeredness and the seeking of one's own honor have no place in Christian discipleship. Rather, Paul urges a kind of letting-go of *ta heautōn*—literally "one's own things"—so that we can give attention to what is important for others. In verse 7 he will characterize this attitude as the kind of "emptying" that was modeled by Christ. It is not that we need to see other believers as "better" than ourselves in the sense of being more virtuous. Rather, Paul is calling for a revaluation in terms of honor: his readers must recognize the value of others (*hyperechontas*—literally, of superior value), and must show them, by serving them and giving them precedence, the honor that is due to them as fellow followers of Christ. This is a way of saying "deny yourselves." Like Christ, we must "step down the social ladder to be a servant."[62] Paul's goal is the promotion of harmony, unity, and peace in the community of believers, which goes along with the Christian graces he mentions in verse 1—encouragement, consolation, love, sharing in the Spirit, compassion, and sympathy. None of these things will be experienced in the presence of selfishness and self-centeredness.

In this passage Paul emphasizes the reciprocal nature of the attitude he is encouraging. The important word *allēlōn* (one another) is used more than sixty times in the New Testament, underlining the mutuality of Christian relationships: love one another, forgive one another, live in harmony with one another, welcome one another, wait for one another, bear one another's burdens, and so on. The exaltation of oneself is incompatible with all of these expressions of unity and harmony. Such self-exaltation is castigated in 2 Tim 3:2—people will be "lovers of themselves."

Verse 5 begins with an imperative: "Think this" (*touto phroneite*). The pronoun "this" probably refers to what Paul has already written in verses 1–4.[63] The verb *phroneite* implies a mind-set (explicit in some translations)

---

61. Rom 2:8; 2 Cor 12:20; Gal 5:20; Phil 1:17; 2:3.

62. Witherington, *Paul's Letter to the Philippians*, 129.

63. Fee, *Paul's Letter to the Philippians*, 199–200.

that Paul wishes his readers to adopt—a cognitive process in which their attitude to themselves is transformed. The subsequent verses describe the attitude of Jesus, using vocabulary that Jesus himself used—as a slave (*doulos*) he humbled himself (*tapeinoō*) and went to the cross; he "emptied himself" (2:7). This act of self-giving is at the heart of the gospel message. When Paul writes, "Let the same attitude be in you," he is asking his readers to "empty themselves" as Jesus did, looking not to their own interests, but to the interests of others (2:4). He seems to be saying that a genuine experience of the *life* of Christ in community depends on the continual transformation of one's attitudes into the *likeness* of Christ,[64] who in selflessness donated himself for the sake of others. Imitation of Christ thus functions as the motivation for the self-denial that Paul teaches in this passage.

A study by Troels Engberg-Pedersen clarifies what Paul means in 2:4. Some translations of this verse say, "Let each of you look *not only* to your own interests, *but also* to the interests of others."[65] Is Paul saying that it is OK to care for ourselves first, and only then to care for others? Engberg-Pedersen points out that there is no "only" in the text, and argues that the *alla kai* in 2:4 does not mean "but also," rather it signals emphasis.[66] This means that Paul's attitude is much more directed to others than to both himself and others. The opposite attitude is highlighted in 2:21, "All of them are seeking their own interests, not those of Jesus Christ." That is, they are not denying themselves. Evidence from the context (especially 2:3, which presents the idea of giving up any consideration for oneself and considering others above oneself) and from other Pauline passages (especially 1 Cor 10:24 and 33) underlines Paul's overriding conviction that "the movement from I to we must always win."[67] This is also seen in 1 Cor 13:5, "*agapē* does not seek its own," and in Rom 12:3, 10, 16; 15:1–3. However, Engberg-Pedersen insists that this attitude is certainly not "abject self-sacrifice."[68] It is not the kind of self-denial that takes no account of oneself. It is not *against* the self; there is no hint of debasing or rejecting the self as such. Paul is concerned, in all the passages referred to, to "establish the perspective of

---

64. Fee, "Philippians 2:5–11," 43.

65. E.g., NASB, ESV, NLT, NET Bible.

66. Engberg-Pedersen, "Radical Altruism," 199–202. Compare 2:4 with 2:27, where Paul does include an "only."

67. Engberg-Pedersen, "Radical Altruism," 205.

68. Engberg-Pedersen, "Radical Altruism," 207.

altruism"—to see oneself just as one among others.[69] I would summarize this by saying that this kind of self-denial is not the denying of one's self in the sense that the self has no worth, but rather it is the relativizing of one's self, which results in the giving of one's self as a donation of great value for the benefit of others.

In 2:19–30 Paul presents to the Philippians two examples of the kind of selfless service he has been writing about. His coworker Timothy has proved that he is "genuinely concerned" for their welfare, not like those who "seek their own interests" (2:19–24). Epaphroditus is also an exemplary Christian, who has risked his life in order to minister to both Paul and the Philippians. Paul says, "Honor such people, because he came close to death for the work of Christ."

Paul's Story of Loss and Gain

In Phil 3 Paul tells something of his own story, and urges his readers to take him as an example. He begins by writing that he puts "no confidence in the flesh." In the context, he is, of course, talking about circumcision: "flesh" here is primarily a reference to what is done to the male body to signify Jewishness. Paul is warning of those false teachers who "have confidence in the flesh" and want to make the non-Jewish Christians undergo Jewish-style circumcision. He makes a distinction between the physically circumcised and the "spiritually circumcised"—those who worship Christ in the Spirit, and do not rely for their identity and security on a physical mark in their body.[70] But after mentioning his own physical circumcision (v. 5) and his ethnic and religious identity as a Jew, he goes on to talk about his behavior—his passion for persecuting Christians, and his flawless observance of religious duties. It seems that Paul includes these things also as part of the "confidence in the flesh" that he has now renounced, so that aspects of the "self"—that is, the "old self"—are components of the "flesh." It seems that this is another way in which he expresses self-denial. He has legitimate grounds for pride and self-congratulation, but he has said *no* to them. He relativizes everything in which he could have boasted—his ethnicity, his Jewish identity symbols, his office, his profession, his zeal, his

---

69. Engberg-Pedersen, "Radical Altruism," 208.

70. Moses told the people of God to "circumcise your hearts" (Deut 10:16); Paul writes that "real circumcision is a matter of the heart—it is spiritual and not literal" (Rom 2:29).

apparent blamelessness, all tokens of honor in the eyes of the worldly court of reputation. He writes further:

> Yet whatever gains I had, these I have come to regard as loss because of Christ. More than that, I regard everything as loss because of the surpassing value of knowing Christ Jesus my Lord. For his sake I have suffered the loss of all things, and I regard them as rubbish, in order that I may gain Christ and be found in him. (Phil 3:7–9)

The repeated use of the word "regard" (*hēgoumai*, three times in vv. 7, 8) implies a cognitively transformed worldview in which everything has been completely revalued.[71] It is hard to imagine a stronger expression of repudiation than the word Paul uses for "rubbish," whether it means dung or merely things cast out for dogs to rummage through. Interestingly, Paul's language of loss and gain recalls the words of Jesus that follow his self-denial saying: "For those who want to save their life will lose it, and those who lose their life for my sake and for the sake of the gospel will save it. For what will it profit them to gain the whole world and forfeit their life?" (Mark 8:35, 36). Paul now lives a new life shaped by his knowledge of Christ—"to live is Christ" (1:21). The gain of this knowledge is his motivation for the renunciation of much that belonged to his former persona, and the "prize of the heavenly call of God in Christ Jesus" is his motivation for "forgetting what lies behind and straining forward to what lies ahead" (3:13, 14). He looks forward to an even better existence: "to die is gain" (1:21). He invites his readers to have the same perspective—"think this" again—and to follow the example that they have seen in his behavior (3:15–17).[72]

One comment on 4:8 is worth making. Paul writes, "Think on these things." His encouragement to take account of "whatever is true, honorable, just, pure. . ." implies that whatever is *not* true, honorable, just, pure and commendable is *not* to be taken account of, and *not* to be dwelt on. We must take control of our thoughts.

1 AND 2 THESSALONIANS

Paul's two brief letters to the thriving young church in Thessalonica make no direct references to self-denial or to ascetic practices as such. However,

---

71. Engberg-Pedersen, "Complete and Incomplete Transformation," 136.

72. Lee, "'Think' and 'Do,'" 639.

on a close reading we find various conventional elements that relate to this theme.

Paul's Self-Affirmation

Paul's presentation of himself is self-affirming without being self-elevating. He asserts that his conduct at Thessalonica was "pure, upright, and blameless" (1 Thess 2:10). He is explicit about his role as apostle (1 Thess 2:7), but, as he explains in greater detail in 1 Cor 9, he has not taken advantage of it by making burdensome demands; rather, he prefers to think of his role as that of a gentle father (1 Thess 2:7, 11), though he calls his readers *adelphoi*—brothers and sisters. And although he can give instructions and commands (1 Thess 4:2; 5:7; 2 Thess 3:4, 10, 12) he has not imposed on them his right to their hospitality, so that he may be a good example of one who works hard (2 Thess 3:8, 9). He does not exalt himself, but works collegially with his coworkers, for throughout these two letters he writes "we" and "our" to represent Silvanus and Timothy (1:1) as well as himself. Their love for the Thessalonian believers is such that they are eager to share "their own selves" (*tas heautōn psychas*) as well as the gospel (1 Thess 2:8).

Suffering for Jesus' Sake

Paul also has much to say about the Thessalonians. Their turning from idols to the "living and true God" (1 Thess 1:9) is counter-cultural—an expression of their renunciation of faith in impotent deities, and their adoption of a new worldview centered on Jesus. It is for this reason that they have suffered for Jesus' sake in the same way as Paul and the Christians in Judea; that is, they have been persecuted and driven out (1 Thess 2:14–15; 2 Thess 1:4). There is no mention of the cross in these two letters, but the reference to Jesus' death (1 Thess 2:15) reminds us of it; the suffering of persecution is exactly what is implied in "taking up the cross" (Mark 8:34).

Saying No to Sexual Immorality

Paul's exhortations in 1 Thess 4:3–8 concern self-control. "Each one of you knows how to control your own body[73] in holiness and honor, not with

---

73. The meaning of *skeuos* in this verse has been controversial even in the earliest

lustful passion, like the Gentiles who do not know God." Specifically, Paul's friends must abstain from *porneia*—they must say *no* to sexual immorality. It is appropriate to ask whether Paul's reference to Gentiles implies a rejection of common practices in his society or a rejection of the Greco-Roman values that may have lain behind such immorality. There is evidence that Paul's sexual morality in fact matched the concern and emphasis of Greco-Roman society in general, for both Cynics and Stoics, like Jews, condemned *porneia*. "While sexual conduct and misconduct were indeed very public and pervasive, the *moral standards* regarding sexual conduct were exacting and high" (emphasis added).[74] Though Paul urges restraint in line with high moral standards held in common with the philosophers and other educated people, he does it for different reasons. The liberal climate made it very easy for Christian believers to fall away from these standards and into (what was to Paul) sin. Moreover, in their new transformed worldview this kind of conduct was out of the question because of the need for holiness (v. 3), which is a foreign concept to those "who do not know God" (v. 5). The basis for self-control of sexual urges is not just conformity to conventional moral standards, but relationship to God, who is mentioned in almost every verse in this passage: it is God himself who calls us to self-control, purity, and righteous behavior (vv. 7–8). This is a call that we must not say *no* to (*atheteō*).

Honor as a Motivation for Self-Denial

These letters mention themes that I have treated elsewhere. Here, as in all his writing, Paul makes much use of the language of honor and shame. Just as we have identified divine honor as a motivation for self-denial in the Gospels, we see evidence of this perspective in the Thessalonian correspondence. Paul writes about his own motives in 1 Thess 2:3–6. Here he makes a strong distinction between traditional sources of honor, which no longer motivate him, and approval by God, who has entrusted to him the proclamation of the gospel. His aim is not to please people, but God. He has renounced self-seeking behavior such as flattery and greed.

---

commentaries. Tertullian and Chrysostom are among those who take it as "body" rather than "wife." The word has the connotation of "body" in 1 Cor 4:7 and 1 Pet 3:7, and in other Greek literature is recognized as a euphemism for the genital organs.

74. Hock, "God's Will," 163.

As for those he is writing to, Paul affirms their new identity: they are beloved and chosen by God (1 Thess 1:4; 2 Thess 2:13). Through their steadfast faith they are already sharing in the glory of God (2 Thess 1:12). Paul earnestly encourages them to ensure that their way of life—their "walk"—is shaped and conditioned by their pursuit of divine honor—that they may be counted "worthy" (*axiōs* in 1 Thess 2:12; *axioō* in 2 Thess 1:5, 11). In other words, the honor that God bestows, as he calls them into his own kingdom and glory, functions as the motivation for this striving. In addition, the necessity for "holiness and honor" motivates self-control in sexual matters (1 Thess 4:4). On the other hand, avoidance of shame is a motivation to obey Paul's instructions and to conform to the expectations of the Christian community (2 Thess 3:15).

TIMOTHY AND TITUS

The letters to Timothy and Titus clearly belong together as a group, despite disagreements as to their authorship. They are the only letters addressed to individuals in positions of church leadership. They are broadly concerned with the same topics: warnings against Hellenistic influences that had infected the churches, and instructions about how Christian leaders should behave both in their personal lives and in their supervision of the congregations. Thus they are called "pastoral" epistles.

Some scholars have claimed that the ethos of these letters is more Hellenistic than in other letters, and that their ethical directives have more the character of Stoic ideas.[75] For example, Christian living is described in terms of godliness and self-control, which are Greek virtues. It is appropriate to ask, then, on what basis does Paul argue for godliness and self-control? He writes that godliness (*eusebeia*) and dignity (*semnotēs*), which are indeed Greek virtues, are "acceptable in the sight of God" (1 Tim 2:2, 3); here and elsewhere he bases the value of the Greek virtues on the character of the "one God" (2:5). All of his instructions ("these things," 1 Tim 4:6) are given on the basis of the "sound teaching" that Timothy has already received and followed. His ethics are drawn, not from Greco-Roman society, but from the Scriptures and his personal experience of the living God (e.g.,

---

75. For example, 1 Tim 3:2–12; 6:6–8; Titus 1:6–8; 2:12. Towner (*Letters*, 326) notes that Paul's view of "progress" (*prokopē*, growth in the practice of moral conduct, e.g., 1 Tim 4:15) and his parenetic style "place him within the sort of didactic framework that shaped the Stoic approach, with certain key nuances . . . needing to be factored in."

1 Tim 4:10; Titus 2:12). The behavior that he urges is that which is required in "the household of the living God" (1 Tim 3:15). Honoring parents and grandparents is "pleasing in God's sight" (1 Tim 5:4). Godliness (*eusebeia*) for Paul is not merely attendance to ritual, or the awareness of religious duties (the "outward form of godliness" without its power, 2 Tim 3:5), but wholehearted devotion to "the blessed and only sovereign, the king of kings and lord of lords" (1 Tim 6:15). His "godly life" is "in Christ Jesus" (2 Tim 3:12) and conforms to "the glorious gospel of the blessed God" (1 Tim 1:11). Philip Towner comments:

> What the Greek ethicists saw as the goal of education, namely, inculcation of Greek "civilization" marked by the cardinal virtues, Paul saw as the jurisdiction of the grace of God in Christ.[76]

Paul's ethical instructions, then, though they share elements recognized and honored in the wider society, are distinctively Christian. Moreover, he is concerned about the church's reputation in the eyes of outsiders, so good behavior is important.

1 TIMOTHY

Saying No to False Teaching

Perhaps the main purpose of 1 Timothy is to counter the false teaching that was a problem in Ephesus. The church was being led astray by some of its own elders. One job of elders was to teach (1 Tim 3:2; 5:17). This explains why there is so much material in Timothy and Titus about the character, qualification, and discipline of church leaders. Paul's presentation of Christian ethics (how to behave) seems to be a direct response to the thinking and behavior of the false teachers; he writes as a teacher of Timothy and Titus.

Paul immediately challenges these deviations. Timothy must teach his people to say *no* to false teachings—to "myths, endless genealogies, speculations" (1 Tim 1:4). These may have been related to how the Old Testament was being used, leading to conjectures based on weird interpretations of passages from the Jewish Scriptures (also Titus 1:14; 3:9) and arguments about the law. Paul denounces not just the cognitive aspects of the false teaching but also the behavior of the false teachers. They speculate, dispute,

---

76. Towner, *Letters*, 208.

argue, and quarrel; they are proud, arrogant, divisive, and fundamentally greedy.

Following Jesus implies avoidance of turning aside from the way. Deviating from the path (like sheep, Isa 53:6) means following one's own inclinations. These must be controlled, and some must be denied. Paul warns that some people in Ephesus have deviated from "a pure heart, a good conscience, and sincere faith" and have turned aside to "meaningless talk," which does not issue from love or promote love (1 Tim 1:3–7). They have not denied themselves, but have given rein to their own interests, assumptions, and dubious beliefs. The end result for such people may be what Paul calls "shipwreck" (19), mentioning Hymenaeus and Alexander as examples. Later in the letter (4:16) Paul encourages Timothy to "pay close attention to yourself" (*epechō*, keep close watch on). In this chapter, he affirms the value of attention to one's heart and one's conscience (1:5). Hymenaeus and Alexander have inappropriately said *no* to their conscience, with disastrous results.

Self-denial does not mean rejecting who you are. In both letters to Timothy, Paul affirms himself as herald, apostle, and teacher (1 Tim 2:7; 2 Tim 1:11). In the second letter, he also affirms his character and his behavior—his faith, patience, love, steadfastness—as well as his persecutions and suffering (2 Tim 3:10–11). However, he has denied his former self, in the sense that he has discarded certain attitudes and practices that pertained to his earlier worldview, when he had "acted ignorantly in unbelief" (1 Tim 1:13), making him, by his own confession, the "foremost" of sinners (15).

Fighting the Good Fight

In 1 Tim 1:18 Paul urges Timothy to "fight the good fight." "Faith and a good conscience" are characteristics of those who are engaged in this struggle (v. 19). The "fight" (*strateia*) perhaps refers to the necessity to oppose false teaching, but the use of a similar expression in 6:12 and 2 Tim 4:7, employing the close synonym *agōn*, seems to require a broader reference. In Greek literature *strateia* can be used figuratively to denote the effort needed to live a moral life,[77] but *agōn*, which has the connotation of an athletic struggle rather than a military one, is often used as a figure for moral and spiritual effort.[78] This is the sense in 6:12, where Paul's appeal to "fight the

77. Johnson, *First and Second Letters*, 185.

78. Johnson, *First and Second Letters*, 306.

good fight" is set in the context of a multitude of imperatives: Timothy is to flee from all kinds of ungodliness, to pursue righteousness, godliness, faith, love, endurance, gentleness (v. 11), to take hold of eternal life, and to maintain a good confession (12, 13). Paul expects that this will require continual strenuous endeavor. It is equivalent to the "training in godliness" that necessitates "toil and struggle," as he writes in 4:7–10. This reminds us that self-discipline (call it self-governance or self-control) is not an easy task. The *agōn* is "against one's own inclinations rather than against the powers of the world."[79] Self-denial, which is a component of self-discipline, implies exertion, determination, and a recognition that there is a battle to be fought, a contest to be won.

Self-Control for Ephesian Women

In 1 Tim 2:9–15 Paul has something to say about how Christian women should exercise self-control. Female readers should be reassured that this passage does not demand denial of their gifts or their womanhood. It must be read in the context of Paul's purpose in these letters. Paul was sensitive to his culture; he wanted to encourage standards of conduct that were consonant with the prevailing first-century social order, and this involved assertion of gender-appropriate behavior that would not provoke controversy or bring disrepute on the Christian community.[80] He wanted the church to "lead a quiet and peaceable life" (2:2). The interpretation of this passage is difficult and still attracts much debate. This is not the place to consider the complexities. However, I will draw attention to some points that may be helpful.

Paul's instructions concerning women come in the context of his instructions about public prayer. These instructions imply the presence of a significant degree of disorder in public worship. Paul seeks to address this: men are to pray (out loud) "without anger or argument" and the women are to do likewise (*hōsautōs*, v. 9), presumably in their leading of public prayer, and to take care that when they do they are dressed modestly and not extravagantly. Paul does not demand that women should be silent in church, for the adjective *hēsuchios* in verse 11 is the same word that is translated as "quiet" or "peaceable" in verse 2; the noun (*hēsuchia*) is used in verse 12 ("quiet" in NIV). Neither does Paul deny that women may

79. Streete, "*Askesis* and Resistance," 307.

80. Streete, "*Askesis* and Resistance," 300.

have teaching gifts, since Priscilla—a teacher, church leader, and helper to Paul—is commended in Rom 16:3–4 and greeted in 2 Tim 4:19. Rather, Paul seems to be addressing a problem regarding the behavior of particular Ephesian women, some of whom (the younger widows) he rebukes in 5:13 for gossiping and lacking restraint in their speech. Paul is here dealing with a historical situation, giving a "temporary restraining order,"[81] not laying down universal principles. He is accommodating to the traditional social structures, to further his (and God's) aim to save all people by bringing them to the knowledge of the truth (2:4).[82] He appeals to his own individual authority—"I desire" (2:8) and "I permit" (2:12)—rather than to the authority of God, and his appeal to the Adam and Eve story (13–15) depends on a somewhat idiosyncratic exegetical strategy. The passage certainly does not mean that self-denial, for women, requires total submission to the will of a male.

Self-Control for Ephesian Leaders

Paul continues in 1 Tim 3 to warn against behaviors that are not appropriate for Christian leaders—the *episkopoi* (1 Tim 3:1–7, also Titus 1:7–9) and the *diakonoi* (3:8–13, also Titus 1:6). The lists of qualifications imply self-control in many areas. Here, though, Paul seems not to be minimizing the value of public esteem, for his language uses multiple expressions of honor: leaders must be above reproach, respectable (3:2, 10; also 5:7), of good reputation with outsiders, so as not to fall into disgrace (7), gaining a good standing (13). In all this, Paul is instructing his people how to conduct themselves (*anastrephesthai*, 15) in the Christian community. Instruction (*parangelia*, 1 Tim 1:3, 5, 18) is necessary because it is so easy to follow one's own inclinations.

Denying False Asceticism

First Timothy 4 continues to warn the believers about those who have gone astray; these have renounced the faith, paying attention to deceitful spirits and demonic teachings; they are hypocrites and liars, with seared consciences (4:1, 2). They include teachers who "forbid marriage and

---

81. Towner, *1–2 Timothy & Titus*, 72.

82. See Vergeer, "Redeemer."

demand abstinence from foods" (4:3). This kind of idea developed in the second century and is clearly expressed in the apocryphal *Acts of Paul and Thecla*, which stresses Paul's asceticism.[83] But in this letter Paul provides a strong warning against inappropriate and excessive asceticism. His argument is based on two considerations: first, these ascetic demands are made by people who do not display the gracious character that would give them authority—in fact, their spirit is antithetical to Christ ("deceitful spirits and teachings of demons," 4:1); and second, the things that they reject (marriage and food) are actually gifts of God, to be received and enjoyed with gratitude.

Working Out in the Spiritual Gym

In 1 Tim 4:7–10 Paul sums up his instruction by urging Timothy to "train himself in godliness" (4:7a). He is well aware that physical training or self-discipline (*gymnasia*) has obvious benefits for our present life, so how much more valuable will discipline in spiritual things be, since this kind of training brings benefits that are not just for now, but also flow into the life to come (4:8). Those of us who regularly go to the gym know that it brings good results, but they come only through hard work—what Paul calls "toil and struggle" (10)—the labor of denying ourselves comfort for a time, in order to reap the reward of better health. For Paul, the "toil and struggle" are worthwhile, because of the end result: "We have set our hope on the living God" and his full salvation. Paul emphasizes the importance of this perspective by adding the double imperative, "Insist on these things and teach them" (11). He adds an exhortation to diligent implementation: "Practice them, devote yourself to them" (15).

He concludes this passage with an exhortation to self-awareness and self-care: "Pay close attention to yourself and to your teaching" (16). Timothy is to have a firm grasp of his identity in Christ and his calling as a pastor. Paul adds, "Continue in these things, for in doing this you will save both yourself and your hearers." The words "save yourself" (*seauton sōseis*) recall Jesus' words in his self-denial saying: "Those who lose their life for my

83. The elements of false teaching mentioned in these letters are similar to those referred to in 1 Corinthians: claims of "knowledge" and "spirituality," over-realized eschatology, denial of sexual relations in marriage (7:1–7), and denial of future bodily resurrection (15:2). Similarly, in Colossae: ascetic practices (Col 2:16–23) and enchantment with wisdom and knowledge (2:2–8) and Old Testament ritual (2:16, 21).

sake, and for the sake of the gospel, will save it (*sōsei autēn*)" (Mark 8:35). Timothy's attentiveness to self-discipline, for the sake of his flock's spiritual nourishment, will lead to salvation for both him and them.

Saying No to Self-Indulgence

First Timothy 5 focuses especially on the treatment of widows. Paul is concerned, not only for appropriate care, but also for the recognition of the damage done by lack of self-control. He presents a strong contrast between those who "set their hope on God" and those who "live for pleasure" (5:5, 6). The latter have allowed their self-indulgent sensual desires to alienate them from Christ (5:11) and this leads to all kinds of trouble (11–13). Again, part of the motivation for self-control is the avoidance of public shame (v. 14, as in 6:1.)

First Timothy 6 returns to the image of "wandering away" from God and the faith (6:10, 21) on account of "senseless and harmful desires" (6:9) including love of money (10). These inner urges are the source of the many vices listed in 6:4–5. Paul urges Timothy to "flee from all this" (11)—to shun the things that would distract and hinder him from following Jesus. Timothy cannot "fight the good fight of faith" (12) unless he has said *no* to his own inclinations and has disciplined himself to pursue righteousness. As an individual, he must control his inner passions, for his consistent practice of godliness is for the sake of the community of believers.

In regard to the wealthy among his people, Paul does not encourage the asceticism of radical renunciation. He urges them to fix their hope on God rather than on "the uncertainty of riches" because God "richly provides us with everything for our enjoyment" (6:17). This surely speaks against any disparagement of legitimate pleasure. He encourages generosity—they are to be "rich in good works" and use their worldly wealth to do good; by doing so, they will be storing up treasure for the future life, the "real" life. There are many Gospel echoes here.

2 TIMOTHY

Paul's second letter to Timothy seems even more urgent than the first, because the situation had not improved, and because of Paul's changed circumstances. This letter is intensely personal. Timothy is to leave Ephesus and come to where Paul is. But in spite of Paul's personal difficulties (he is in prison) and the great concern he has for the problems in Ephesus, Paul is confident that God will remain faithful and that the gospel and the church will survive.

The Flip Side of Self-Denial

He is quick to remind Timothy about the gifts God has given to him and to all believers (2 Tim 1:6, 7). The flip side of self-denial (in the sense of putting off the old self) is the acceptance of the new self that comes with the new life of faith. This includes self-control, or self-discipline (*sōphronismos*, v. 7). The "spirit of self-control" is a gift bestowed—it is a God-given grace that does not come naturally. Timothy is to rely on this gift, and the power of the Spirit that goes with it (v. 8), so that there is no need to be ashamed of proclaiming the gospel or suffering for it. The fear that makes one timid prevents faithful discipleship.

Shamed but Not Ashamed

In 2 Tim 1 honor and shame language appears in conjunction with theological underpinnings of discipleship. We are told that Paul has suffered the betrayal of his fellow-workers in the province of Asia (1:15). Phygelus and Hermogenes are named here, but later (4:10, 14–16) he says more. He has experienced many of the consequences of self-denial that Jesus foretold in the gospels, including imprisonment (2:9) and persecutions (3:11, 12). But he endures all this hardship for the sake of those he cares about (2:10).[84] He is not self-focused but other-focused. He suffers not for himself but out of consideration for his people; he is dedicated to their salvation and future glory. From a worldly point of view, Paul himself has suffered shame, but he is not ashamed (1:12). Rather, he is confident of himself and his ministry, because both are firmly founded on the fact that God has called him and equipped him. Onesiphorus (1:16) has not been ashamed of Paul's imprisonment; neither is Timothy to be ashamed of Paul, or ashamed to testify about the Lord Jesus (1:8). Paul tells him to be diligent to present himself to God as a workman who does not need to be ashamed; he is to seek God's approval (2:15). Notice that Paul uses the "deny" word in 2:12 and 13—"If

---

84. This use of *dia* ("for the sake of") is another example of motivation that is future-oriented (see ch. 2).

we deny him, he will also deny us." This takes us right back to Mark 8:38, where Jesus says, "Those who are ashamed of me and of my words . . . of them the Son of Man will also be ashamed."

The Hard Work of Self-Discipline

In 2 Tim 2:3–6 Paul presents three metaphors without interpreting them. First, Timothy is to be "a good soldier." The implication of the image is that those who are following Christ (the one who enlisted them) should aim to please him, rather than "getting entangled" in pursuits that are not relevant or appropriate to the endeavor. The self-discipline of Christian "soldiers" means that they will often have to say *no*, and suffer as a result. The second is the athlete metaphor, which Paul uses elsewhere (e.g., 1 Cor 9:24–27). An athlete requires determination and self-discipline in order to compete "according to the rules." The third image is of the farmer, who cannot enjoy his produce without much hard work. In each of the three metaphors, the goal supplies the motivation for the striving.[85] Paul's charge to Timothy is to "do your best to present yourself approved (*dokimos*) to God as a workman who does not need to be ashamed, accurately handling the word of truth" (2:15).[86] It is clear that Paul wants his coworker to be diligent—to make every effort—motivated by the prospect of approval and honor from God. For this, he needs to be trained. *Paideia* (training, 2:16) is an ongoing process that requires not only the right equipment (here it's the Scriptures) but commitment and determination, where certain aspects of one's personal agenda must often take second place.

When to Say No and When to Say Yes

Paul helps Timothy to recognize things to say *no* to. There are lists of vices in this chapter and the next: "profane chatter" (2:16), "youthful passions" (2:22), "senseless controversies" (2:23), and so on. Timothy must avoid these things, turn aside from them, and have nothing to do with them. Followers of Jesus need to "cleanse themselves" from these dishonorable things (2:21), many of which Paul has mentioned in his first letter (1 Tim

---

85. Towner, *Letters*, 495.

86. The word for "do your best" (*spoudazō*) is used four times in these letters: here and in 4:9; 4:21; and Titus 3:12.

6:4–5). Here he mentions many more, piling nineteen adjectives and nouns together in a vast catalogue of sins and sinners (3:2–5). He predicts that "in the last days . . . people will be lovers of themselves" as well as lovers of money (3:2), like Demas, who is "in love with this present world" (4:10). They will be lovers of pleasure rather than lovers of God (3:4). They will say *no* (*arneomai*) to the power of godliness while appearing to display it (3:5, cf. Titus 1:16). Giving priority to "their own desires," they will forsake sound teaching and turn away from the truth, following myths instead (4:3, 4).

Rejecting all this, Timothy is to say *yes* to the graces and virtues that are acceptable to God: righteousness, faith, love, and peace (2:22)—in addition to those he has already mentioned in his first letter—godliness, endurance, gentleness, generosity (1 Tim 6:11, 18).

TITUS

Paul's letter to Titus warns against the threat of false teaching. His theme here is encouragement to help people live exemplary Christian lives for the sake of outsiders. It's all about character and behavior. There are many good qualities to pursue (e.g., 2:2–5), and plenty of bad ones to avoid, deny, and renounce.

Saying No to the Wrong Things

Paul uses the "deny" word (*arneomai*) in relation to people in Crete who give no evidence of being believers, though they claim to be. "They profess to know God, but they deny him by their actions" (Titus 1:16). They have said *no* to the wrong thing. In contrast, Paul stresses the necessity for real believers to "say 'no' (*arneomai*) to ungodliness and worldly passions" (Titus 2:12 NIV). Rather, they must live lives that are self-controlled (*sōphronōs*), upright (*dikaiōs*), and godly (*eusebōs*). Paul lays emphasis on the importance of self-control throughout this short letter, using forms of *sōphrōn* in 2:2, 5, 6, 12, the synonym *enkrateia* in 1:8, and *nēphalios* in 2:2. The word *nēphalios* means sober, temperate (also in 1 Tim 3:2, 11). This may refer to avoidance of drunkenness, but the root verb *nēphō* (2 Tim 4:5; 1 Thess 5:6, 8; 1 Pet 1:13; 4:7; 5:8) has a wider meaning that includes self-control, self-restraint, and self-possession.

Imperatives of this kind are found throughout Paul's writings; they imply the necessity of some degree of self-denial, since self-governance necessarily requires saying *no* to some persistent human tendencies that are incompatible with following Christ. I think it is fair to say that self-denial and self-governance are related activities, which may be practiced with a variety of perspectives and motivations. Paul's motivation for denying "worldly passions" arises, of course, from his relationship to Christ, rather than from a concern for self-improvement.[87] He confesses the bad attitudes he has had in the past, including "slavery to various passions and pleasures" (3:3). He has had to deny this servitude, and to control his desires, but he attributes his transformation not to himself but to the mercy of God in Christ his savior, and his renewal by the Holy Spirit (3:4–7).

Eschatological Hope as a Motivation for Self-Denial

Some of the New Testament documents provide explicit reasons for denying oneself, but in others the motivation is more implicit. Like the Gospels, the Pauline letters affirm that the prospect of eschatological honor is a strong incentive for vigorous attention to one's attitudes and behavior. Eschatological motivation is present in all three letters to Timothy and Titus. The future coming of Christ in glory is anticipated using a variety of language. The prospect of "that day" (2 Tim 1:12, 18; 4:8) inspires perseverance in suffering, and is the implied motivation for running the race and fighting the good fight. Timothy is to proclaim the gospel "in view of [Christ's] appearing and his kingdom" (2 Tim 4:1). The expectation of riches in the future life motivates the godly use of wealth in this age (1 Tim 6:19). Godliness is valuable because it "holds promise for both the present life and the life to come" (1 Tim 4:8). The motivation for faithful endurance of suffering is the assurance of obtaining salvation "with eternal glory" and that "we will also reign with him" (2 Tim:10–12). "The blessed hope and the manifestation of the glory of our great God and Savior Jesus Christ" inspires the living of self-controlled, godly lives (Titus 2:12, 13). These references are expansions of what Paul has mentioned in passing in other letters. He "dies daily" as he "puts himself in danger every hour" because he

---

87. For a detailed examination of the differences between the treatment of ethical virtues in Titus and Greco-Roman literature, see Christensen, "Pursuit of Self-Control." "The primary accommodation being asked of the believing community is to deny selfish ambition in steadfast pursuit of Christ" (180).

is certain of bodily resurrection (1 Cor 15:30–31). For believers generally, the shortness of time and the imminence of the coming age (1 Cor 7:29, 31) require reconsideration of one's needs, desires, and priorities.

PHILEMON

Paul writes to his friend and fellow worker Philemon with an appeal. Onesimus, presumably Philemon's slave, has come to Paul, who is sending him back to his master with the letter. Although the letter does not give us all the details of the story, it evidences two examples of self-denial. First, Paul relinquishes this own desire to keep Onesimus with him (v. 13) because of his greater desire for reconciliation between these brothers in Christ, his sense of duty to Philemon, and his conviction that his advice, if taken, will be to Philemon's advantage.[88]

Secondly, Paul encourages Philemon to overrule his rights as a slave owner and to accept his slave as a Christian brother. Masters regarded their slaves as pieces of property, and could exercise total control over them, so that Philemon would be within his rights in punishing Onesimus in whatever way he wished. However, on the basis of Onesimus' transformation through his acceptance of the gospel, Paul appeals to Philemon to say *no* to cultural expectations, and to welcome the slave back in a spirit of forgiveness and brotherhood.

IMITATION AS SELF-DENIAL IN PAUL'S LETTERS

The rhetoric of imitation in the New Testament urges readers to adopt attitudes and patterns of behavior modeled by someone else. To the extent that such intentional adoption overrides one's own inclinations, imitation is a form of self-denial. I think it is true to say that to imitate someone implies: (i) the worthiness of that person to be regarded as an example to follow; (ii) a recognition that in oneself there are things that need to be changed, to be handled differently, to be transformed; and (iii) a conscious choice to subordinate one's own inclinations to the pursuit of the worthier goals and practices that are exemplified in the one being imitated. Taking someone else as an example to follow necessarily means acknowledging that they have certain values and characteristics that we lack and need, but it may

---

88. Witherington, *Letters*, 78.

also mean confessing that we need to make changes to the attitudes and actions to which we are accustomed. Saying *yes* to the better way of another person means saying *no* to the way we have always done things.

To "follow Jesus" implies at least some degree of imitation. Jesus trained his disciples by sending out the Twelve and the 72 to "proclaim the kingdom of God and to heal" (Luke 9:2; 10:1–12), that is, to do the kinds of things he himself did, even to "take up the cross." Followers of Jesus are to go where he leads, and they are to do what he does. Jesus himself imitated God: "Whatever the Father does, the Son does likewise. . . . I seek to do not my own will but the will of him who sent me" (John 5:19, 30). Jesus urged his followers to imitate God by striving to be "perfect" (Matt 5:48) and "merciful" (Luke 6:36). His words echo the Old Testament directive to "walk in the ways of the Lord" (Deut 8:6; 10:12; and others).

The apostle Paul, as a disciple of Jesus, consciously imitated him (1 Cor 11:1) and encouraged his readers to do the same. The richest example of this is Phil 2:1–11, urging the attitude of humility that Christ showed. Paul also points to Christ's generosity—"Though he was rich, yet for your sakes he became poor" (2 Cor 8:9)—and declares that "Christ did not please himself" (Rom 15:3). Imitation also implies sharing in Christ's death through suffering (Phil 1:29; 3:10). There is no thoroughgoing self-denial without a willingness to suffer on account of faith in him.

Much has been written on the "imitation of Christ." Richard Burridge stresses that imitation of Christ is not about copying, but about taking Christ as the ethical model—it is about moral character.[89] Gordon Fee writes that we "are not called upon simply to 'imitate God' by what we do, but to have this very mind, the mind of Christ, developed in us, so that we too bear God's image in our attitudes and relationships within the Christian community and beyond."[90] This is what Paul means when he urges his readers to take himself as an example.[91] Anthony Thiselton helpfully points out that when Paul writes "Be imitators of me" (1 Cor 11:1) he does not mean it in the sense of replication, but in the sense of following a pattern or broad model of attitudes and behavior.[92] Paul's exhortations to imitate himself have been criticized by some skeptical postmodern scholars[93] as

---

89. Burridge, *Imitating Jesus*.

90. Fee, "Philippians 2:5–11," 45.

91. 1 Cor 4:16; 11:1; Phil 3:17; 4:9; 2 Thess 3:7–9; 1 Tim 1:16.

92. Thiselton, *First Corinthians*, 166.

93. E.g., Castelli, *Imitating Paul.*

requiring conformity, and as a means of manipulation and control of his communities. This view is easily refuted if we accept as honest and guileless Paul's many statements of his intentions and motivations—that Christ be preeminent in his life and in the lives of his communities. According to Paul, the Thessalonian believers imitated both him and Christ, and themselves became examples to believers in other places (1 Thess 1:6–7).

Eph 5:1–2 also urges us to be "imitators of God" by "living in love, as Christ loved us." This recalls the words of Jesus in Matt 5:48, "Be perfect, as your heavenly Father is perfect." The context of this saying indicates that Jesus was referring to imitating the impartial love of God, which extends beyond neighbors, even to enemies, and thus demands relinquishment of our natural tendencies to fear and avoid those who do not love us. Not far from this is the command in Lev 19:2, "You shall be holy, for I the Lord your God am holy." Here God tells Moses of his desire for his people to be like God. The biblical definition of humanity as those who are made "in the image of God" implies a close correspondence between the human character and the divine character. The distortion of human nature has fractured this correspondence. Self-denial means working consciously against the pressure of this fracture. As we say *no* to the temptation to autonomy and self-exaltation, and set our hearts to be more like God, the image of God in us is progressively restored.

LOVE FOR ONE ANOTHER AS SELF-DENIAL IN PAUL'S LETTERS

Love is both a motivation for self-denial and an expression of self-denial. In terms of motivation, Paul bases his appeal for transformation of individuals and the community of believers on the demonstration of God's love. The love of God for sinful humans is highlighted several times in Romans, as an important component of Paul's great "indicative" exposition: "God's love has been poured into our hearts . . . God proves his love for us . . ." (Rom 5:5, 8); "nothing in all creation will be able to separate us from the love of God in Christ Jesus our Lord" (Rom 8:35–39). And Paul bases his imperative to "put to death the deeds of the body" (Rom 8:13) on the new relationship of love in which believers have become adopted children of the Father (Rom 8:14–17). Then in 2 Cor 5:14 and 15 "the love of Christ urges us on" so that we might live no longer for ourselves. Our transformation is energized by this love, as we are "being rooted and grounded in love . . . the love of Christ" (Eph 3:17, 19).

Love is also an expression of self-denial, in the sense that love requires a shift of focus away from ourselves. I mentioned above that "one another" appears more than sixty times in the New Testament, emphasizing the mutuality of Christian relationships. In the Thessalonian letters, for example, Paul insists that his friends must love one another (1 Thess 3:12; 4:9; 2 Thess 1:3) by encouraging one another, building one another up, and doing good to one another (1 Thess 4:18; 5:11, 15). Paul tells the Galatians to deny self-indulgence, and instead "through love become slaves to one another" (Gal 5:13). Paul's emphasis on the priority of love is obvious, of course, in the wonderful exposition of love in 1 Cor 13, to which we drew attention above. Just as comprehensive, though less poetic, is his explanation of what love looks like in Rom 12:9–21, but elsewhere he opts for short, all-encompassing statements: "Owe no-one anything, except to love one another" (Rom 13:8) and "Let all that you do be done in love" (1 Cor 16:14). However, he is quite specific in linking the attitudes and actions of love to certain situations in which self-denial is appropriate. "Love builds up" in the context of denying oneself certain foods for the sake of others (1 Cor 8:1), and regarding the necessity for self-control in public meetings of believers, the Corinthians are to "pursue love" (1 Cor 14:1). "Let love be genuine," writes Paul in the context of recognizing the gifts of others, and not thinking of oneself too highly (Rom 12:9), and denying oneself things that cause others to stumble (Rom 14:13–21) is "walking in love" (14:15).

Ephesians is particularly rich in love language. In Eph 4, which calls for the maintenance of unity within the Christian community, self-denial is strongly implied, as independence and self-focus is relinquished for the sake of others. Believers "bear with one another in love" as the body is "building itself up in love" (Eph 4:2, 16). Growth in maturity means "speaking the truth in love" (Eph 4:15). As we learn to say *no* to bad attitudes (Eph 4:31–32) we "live in love, as Christ loved us" (Eph 5:2). A special passage (Eph 5:25–33) tells husbands to love their wives, "just as Christ loved the church" (5:25) and just as they love their own bodies (5:28). Love for the spouse is paralleled both by Christ's love for us and by love for oneself. Thus the quality of our love for others is such that we must "nourish and tenderly care for" them.

PAUL AS AN EXAMPLE OF SELF-DENIAL

Before exploring the rest of the New Testament, we should note, in summary, some aspects of Paul's example as a practitioner of self-denial. In Paul's writings there is a strong emphasis on the subjugation of personal interests for the sake of Christ and the gospel. An important foundation for this is Paul's recognition of the ways in which God has honored his people through the work of Christ. Paul, as a disciple and imitator of Jesus, "takes up the cross daily," conscious of his losses but fully persuaded of the greater worth of following Christ.

If we compare the attitudes and lives of Paul and Jesus, we can detect several parallels. Though his letters do not use the language of "following Christ" it is clear that Paul was indeed a faithful follower, describing himself as an imitator of Christ (1 Cor 11:1). He taught "in every church" his "ways of life in Christ" (1 Cor 4:17). Both said *no* to aspects of their humanity because of their commitment to the reign of God. Christian Wolff identifies some characteristics of their lives that demonstrate self-denial: they both suffered deprivation, they both renounced marriage, they were both engaged in humble service, and they were both persecuted for their selfless conformity to God's ways.[94] In the words of Tom Wright, Jesus and Paul "were at one in the basic vision which generated their very different vocations."[95]

Paul mentions his poverty and homelessness in 1 Cor 4:11–12, and his periods of hunger and lack of clothing in 2 Cor 6:5 and 11:27. In one sense we could say that these deprivations and other sorts of suffering were due to the forces of circumstance, for he did not choose them. However, because he had been gripped by the power of the risen Christ, and for the sake of obedience to his call to preach the gospel, and because of his love for the family of God, he did choose not to pursue wealth and the stability of a settled home and marriage. He makes no mention of his own family of origin, but one wonders whether his lists of trials include veiled references to exclusion by his natural family.

As a self-conscious disciple of Jesus, he was enabled and motivated to self-deny—to endure dishonor in the eyes of the world—by his experience of grace—the honor that Christ had bestowed on him—and was urged on

94. See Wolff, "Humility and Self-Denial." Wolff writes (160) that "there are some "remarkable correspondences . . . but it is impossible to discover from Paul's letters whether the apostle was conscious of them."

95. Wright, *Paul*, 161.

in this resolve by the anticipation of eschatological honor. Paul provides a theology of self-affirmation and self-denial based on a new vision of the ways in which honor flows in Christian community. He urges self-denial on the basis of honor lavished on the community by God. This creation of a new identity, founded on a radical reordering of relationships with God, family, and church ("fictive family") enables followers of Christ to "put off the old self."

PAUL AND THE CROSS OF CHRIST

"Taking up the cross" is an integral component of Jesus' "self-denial" saying. We might ask the question, Does Paul say anything that corresponds to the expression "taking up the cross"? Of course, Paul mentions the cross many times, for it stands at the very center of his message (1 Cor 1:18; 2:2), but in some of these references Paul connects the cross to himself in a very personal way. He has been persecuted for the cross of Christ (Gal 6:12)—so much so that he writes, "I bear on my body the marks (*stigmata*) of Jesus" (Gal 6:17). He has "participated in the sufferings of Christ, becoming like him in his death" (Phil 3:10). Referring to the dangers he faces "every hour," he writes, "I die daily" (1 Cor 15:31), using the phrase *kath hēmeran*, which takes us to Jesus' words in Luke 9:23, "let them take up their cross *daily* and follow me." He provides long lists of his sufferings in 2 Cor 6:4–10 and 11:23–33—floggings, stonings, imprisonments, and various kinds of affliction and deprivation. This identification with the sufferings of Jesus is explicit also in 2 Cor 13:4—"He was crucified in weakness, yet he lives by God's power; likewise, we are weak in him, yet by God's power we will live with him." Paul's identification with the sufferings of Christ becomes even more graphic in passages where he speaks figuratively of being "crucified with Christ" (Rom 6:6 and Gal 2:20). One aspect of his "self" is now dead through identification with Christ on the cross. The "old self" (*ho palaios anthrōpos*), the old way of life dominated by sin, has been rendered powerless, so that he is set free from sin's bondage. "We have been united with him in a death like his, and we will certainly be united with him in a resurrection like his" (Rom 6:5). Paul applies this concept to himself in Gal 6:14—through the cross of Christ, which is his "only boast," Paul has been "crucified to the world." Through his identification with the death of Jesus, Paul has made a radical break with "the world," that is, his former way of life, the "old world of inherited advantages and achieved successes"[96] that he catalogues elsewhere.

96. Fung, *Epistle to the Galatians*, 307.

CHAPTER 4

Self-Denial in the General Letters and Revelation

HEBREWS

The letter to the Hebrews was written by an unknown author for the purpose of encouraging followers of Jesus to maintain their commitment to discipleship in a cultural environment that did not support Christianity, and was in many ways hostile to it. The recipients of the letter had been "exposed to abuse and persecution" and had experienced "plundering of their possessions" (10:32–34) because of their faith. Much of the letter—the first ten and a half chapters—is given to Christology. The author builds a picture of Jesus as creator and sustainer of the world, Son of God, and great high priest, who himself has mediated a new covenant through the shedding of his own blood for the forgiveness of sins and is now seated at God's right hand. All of this lays the firmest of foundations for the exhortations given in chapters 10–13. Because of the supremacy of Christ and the superiority of his achievements, any turning back from following him—any refusal to persevere in discipleship, despite the difficulties—is unthinkable.

"Despising the Shame"

Hebrews 11, especially vv. 35–38, lists many hardships experienced by faithful Israelites. There is self-denial here, manifested in refusal to submit to evil. Release from torture would have been an attractive proposition, but they refused to take the easy way out. The author is probably referring to pre-Christian worshipers of God, especially those who suffered at the time of the Maccabees, who would not have known Jesus' saying, that "those who want to save their life will lose it" (Mark 8:35). Nevertheless, they lived (and died) in accordance with the principle. Giving in would mean that they valued their human life more than eternal life; they looked forward to a resurrection that would be even "better" than receiving back their mortal life (11:35). The author commends these faithful people for their perseverance under trial; he writes that they are those "of whom the world was not worthy" (11:38, 39). This statement subverts the world's system of values and, in effect, disgraces and invalidates that system.

Recalling our discussion of honor as a motivation for self-denial in the Gospels, it is helpful to recognize that in Hebrews there is a high incidence of vocabulary and concepts related to honor and dishonor.[1] Among these are *doxa* (glory), *timē* (honor), *axios* (worthy), *kreittōn* (better), *aischunē* (disgrace, shame), *oneidismos* (reproach), *hubrizō* (insult, mistreat), and others. Jesus "endured the cross, disregarding its shame" (12:2); that is, Jesus gave no value to the opinions of the dominant culture. David deSilva has shown that the letter to the Hebrews employs the rhetoric of honor and shame to encourage the Christian group to persevere in their discipleship despite the shame of it. Finding themselves in a situation of dishonor in the eyes of society, they are urged to despise this shame, as Jesus did (12:2), and to embrace "the reproach of Christ" (11:26; 13:13). DeSilva writes that Jesus chose "to embrace a lower status in the eyes of the society in order to pursue the greater and lasting honor to be won through obedience to God."[2] "One either honors and obeys God at the risk of dishonoring and provoking the world, or one honors and conforms to society at the risk of dishonoring and provoking God."[3]

By these means, the author urges the readers to step out of the system of honor that belongs to the unbelieving society—to disregard their opinions—and cling to the honor they have in God's sight and in the sight of fellow believers, who together make up the alternative court of reputation.

---

1. See deSilva, *Despising Shame.*
2. DeSilva, *Bearing Christ's Reproach,* 38.
3. DeSilva, *Hope of Glory,* 153.

Running the Race

Heb 12 echoes in several ways the themes of discipleship and cross-bearing. Why should we follow Jesus? In the first part of the book the answer has been, "because Jesus is a better priest." Now the author uses two different rhetorical strategies to encourage Christian readers to endure the suffering that they experience as Christ-followers.

The first is about running the race. Heb 12:1–2 is a call to self-discipline. The writer uses the athletic image of the running race.[4] It is goal-centered, for the followers of Jesus look to him, who has already finished his race despite much difficulty and opposition. "Despising the shame" is a clever use of honor language. The writer acknowledges that Jesus experienced the ultimate public shame of crucifixion. However, this dishonor is matched and neutralized by Jesus' attitude: he scorned the dishonor heaped on him, he shamed the shame. The writer certainly envisages similar kinds of hostility directed toward his readers, and encourages them toward a similar attitude—there will be public shame for being a Christian, but the experience of dishonor and shame will not be worth taking much notice of. It will be powerless to hinder the believers in their race toward Jesus.

What they are called to is described in several ways. They are to "lay aside (*apotithēmi*, throw off, be done with) every weight and the sin that so easily entangles us" (12:1), saying *no* to burdens and encumbrances that do not help to maintain the life of discipleship. They are called to endurance (*hupomonē*, steadfastness, perseverance, 12:2, 3) and resistance (*antikathistēmi*), even to the point of shedding blood in the struggle to say *no* to sin (12:4). "For the sake of the joy that was set before him" (12:2) echoes the eschatological perspective that often functions as motivation in these exhortations to perseverance and self-denial. "We are looking for the city that is to come" (13:14).

The second rhetorical strategy is to urge an acceptance of God's discipline. The readers are encouraged to view the sufferings they experience in following Christ as non-punitive *paideia* (instruction, training, or

---

4. Croy (*Endurance in Suffering*) helpfully examines Heb 12:1–13 in great detail. Croy situates the passage "in the broad context of the *agōn* motif in Hellenistic moral teaching," and demonstrates that "the specific language of the passage, viewed alongside similar expressions in Greco-Roman comparative texts, supports a primarily athletic interpretation" (42). Athletic imagery is present in "let us run the race," "putting off every weight," "endurance," "fatigued . . . weary," and perhaps "cloud of witnesses," also "forerunner" in 6:20.

discipline) that comes from God's hand. This word, in various forms, is used in every verse from 5 to 11. Like Paul, the author of this passage makes much rhetorical use of the father-child image: God treats the followers of Jesus as God's children. As Jesus' cross-bearing provides the motivation for his followers' perseverance in difficulties, the Father's love, expressed as *paideia*, provides comfort and assurance in distressing circumstances, which are to be expected because of following Jesus. There is a *qal wahomer*[5] argument here: if the discipline of human parents is respected (9a), much more so the discipline of the divine Father, which leads to life, holiness, and peace (9b–11). "Discipline always seems painful rather than pleasant at the time, but later it yields the peaceful fruit of righteousness to those who have been trained by it" (12:11).

At 12:12–13 the author returns to the athletic image: "Therefore, lift your drooping hands and strengthen your weak knees, and make straight paths for your feet." The last phrase is a quotation from the LXX version of Prov 4:26, which, in its context, makes it clear that we have choices to make about our running. Self-denial involves the choice *not* to look in certain directions, and *not* to turn our feet onto dangerous or dubious paths (Prov 4:25–27).

Before leaving Hebrews, we must note the author's exhortations to love one another: "Let us think of ways to motivate one another to acts of love and good deeds . . . encouraging one another" (10:24, 25 NLT). And again, using the evocative word *philadelphia*: "Let mutual love continue" (13:1). This attitude is necessarily other-focused, and so requires abandonment of an exclusive self-focus. Some examples follow: showing hospitality to strangers, and empathizing with those in prison or under persecution (13:3).

JAMES

James gives special attention to the negative aspects of anthropology. Many imperatives in this letter counsel self-control and imply self-denial in the sense that they urge attention to God and others, beyond self-absorption. For example, asking God for wisdom (1:5) implies giving up one's self-reliance, and allowing God to have the central place in one's life. The whole letter is based on the assumption that to exalt oneself or to rely on one's

5. The Hebrew expression *qal wahomer* means "light to heavy" and so is equivalent to "how much more."

natural inclinations is ultimately futile, whereas a blessed and joyful life issues from submission to God. Like the Gospels and Hebrews, this letter uses the language of honor and shame. Believers who persevere under testing will be approved (*dokimos*) by God, and will receive the crown of life (1:12). Those who are faithful will be blessed (*makarios*) in all they do (1:12, 25). They have been called by the honorable name of God (2:7), who shows favor (*charis*) to the humble (4:6). And as in the Gospels, the motivation for self-denial and submission to God in this letter is the prospect of eschatological honor: "the Lord's coming is near" (5:7–9) when the faithful will be judged and approved.

Avoiding Self-Deception

In 1:13–16 James begins to write about what the human heart is really like. "Don't be deceived," he warns in 1:16. He doesn't want his readers to have any false ideas about human nature. Though he mentions later that all people are made in the image of God (3:9), James highlights the negative aspects of our humanity: we are sinful. Here he singles out our evil desires, which lure us into wrong thinking and destructive acting, giving birth to sin and even to death. Later he says we are defiled (3:6), ephemeral (4:14), proud and self-centered (4:1–10), with tongues that need to be tamed (3:8). He calls for resistance to these personal vices for which we as individuals are ultimately responsible. "Don't be deceived," he writes, but he is primarily interested to warn against self-deception. To deceive oneself is to deny what is real, and consequently self-deception invalidates attempts at self-denial. James gives two examples of self-deception: we deceive ourselves if we think that hearing the word is enough, without putting it into practice (1:22), and we can have a false perception of ourselves if we think we are religious yet are not in control of our tongues (1:26).

Receiving the Word of God

"Rid yourselves of all sordidness and rank growth of wickedness" (1:21). Here James calls for the kind of self-denial that is better specified as self-discipline and self-governance. This is a call to "put off" not just unwholesome speech but a broad range of impure behavior. In place of the things thrown off, the gifts of God are to be received, especially the "implanted word"—the "word of truth" (1:18) through which new life is obtained.

The "perfect law of liberty" (1:25) seems to refer to the word of God, the revelation received from the Spirit and implanted in the heart (Jer 31:33–34). This is not the Law that enslaves us, as Paul writes. We do not need to be saved from this law—it is the teaching of Christ that we must put into practice. It is the "royal law" that emphasizes love (2:8), the "law of Christ" that requires us to carry each other's burdens (Gal 6:2). It is the "law of freedom" because it sets us free from ourselves (our self-interest, our self-absorption) in order to serve others. It is the moral and ethical teaching of Christ, based on the Old Testament moral law, as embodied in the Ten Commandments but fulfilled and perfected by Christ. It is perfect because it reveals the perfect will of God—it gives undistorted revelation about ourselves and about God.

Avoiding the Pollution of the "World"

James urges believers to keep themselves from being "stained by the world" (1:27). The word James uses for "world" is *kosmos*. This can mean, in a spatial sense, the physical cosmos—that is, the whole of creation—but for most of the New Testament writers the "world" takes on the sense of being in opposition to the "world to come," that is, the kingdom of God. The "world" is transitory, and hostile to God. John tells us that Jesus "was in the world, and the world came into being through him, yet the world did not know him" (John 1:10). The "world" necessarily nurtures us and shapes us, yet also spoils us and stains us—this is a fact of life. Many believers have tried to escape its influence by retreating from society and establishing a separate alternative existence in hermitages and monasteries, where they can hopefully lead a pure and unpolluted life. But James does not encourage this. He assumes that followers of Jesus will be fully active in the everyday business of ordinary life. However, it is difficult to "keep oneself from being stained by the world," hence James' encouragement to do so. James is echoing here the perspective that Jesus articulated: we are "in the world, but not of it" (John 17:14–16).

Controlling the Tongue

Actions arise from attitudes, and attitudes are expressions of the self. Speech is a clear indicator of moral and spiritual character. James is concerned to emphasize the wisdom of self-control in the use of the tongue. He visits this theme several times, first in 1:19–20, then in 1:26; 3:1–12; and 4:11–12. "Let everyone be quick to listen, slow to speak, slow to anger, for your anger does not produce God's righteousness" (1:19–20). This sounds very like the many proverbs in the Bible about control of the tongue, such as Prov 10:19, "The wise hold their tongues." Holding one's tongue is a form of self-control, by which it is appropriate to say *no* to expressing negative emotions or selfish thoughts—behavior should not be controlled by emotions. The tongue needs to be "bridled" if it is to be a witness to "religion that is pure and undefiled" (1:26–27). James explains the image of the bridle and illustrates his point by adding other metaphors in 3:1–12—the tongue is like the rudder of a ship, or a fire that can become wild and do great damage. The tongue is especially difficult to control; this is why we need wisdom for knowing when to speak and when to be silent. Often silence is more powerful than speech.

James' illustrations from nature in 3:10–12 remind us of Jesus' words: "Out of the abundance of the heart the mouth speaks" (Matt 12:34). Since the words that come out of our mouths reveal what is in our hearts, control of the tongue implies the necessity for control of our thoughts and attitudes. Self-control (a fruit of the Spirit) acknowledges our emotions but does not allow them to direct our lives. Nor does it allow us to disrupt the community of believers by "speaking evil against one another" (4:11–12), by which James implies that we should say *no* to slander, condemnation of others, gossip, and any other kinds of talk that do not fulfill "the royal law of love" (2:8). The speech of Jesus-followers must be in submission to God and his word.

Denying Self-Focus

In 3:14–17 James goes on to describe sinful attitudes that come from what may seem to be "wisdom" but is not godly wisdom. His main attack is on "bitter envy and selfish ambition" (14, 16) as the root causes of trouble. They are natural inclinations (*eipgeios*, "earthly," and *psychikē*, "unspiritual") but they are self-focused. James also uses the word *daimoniōdēs*, "demonic," to characterize these attitudes as entirely opposed to the character of God. They are aspects of self that followers of Christ must say *no* to.

Envy is described here as "bitter" because bitterness is a metaphor for tragedy, pain, and grief. Bitter water in the Old Testament was stagnant water, unfit for drinking. Here it describes a polluted, distorted attitude. It's the attitude mentioned in the Ten Commandments: "You shall not covet your neighbor's house, wife, etc." The word for "selfish ambition" is the Greek word *eritheia*. I mentioned previously that this word stands for the exact opposite of self-denial. Of course, ambition can be a good thing: if we have a good goal, we want to succeed for a good purpose. There is a drive to create, achieve, and conquer obstacles. But selfishness means that we are acting purely in our own interest, for what we can get out of it, to enhance our own position, without respect for anyone else. This is foolish, because it puts Self at the center, not God. What James encourages is the "humility that comes from wisdom" (3:13 NIV).

Wisdom is the theme of verse 17. Godly wisdom (that is, wisdom that is characteristic of God) is described with words that really apply to people, not wisdom itself. James gives a list of eight qualities or virtues that describe a wise, righteous person: "The wisdom from above is first pure, then peaceable, gentle, willing to yield, full of mercy and good fruits, without a trace of partiality or hypocrisy." These are qualities that it is appropriate to embrace and choose as one's way of life. Paul, noting that many of these qualities are aspects of love (1 Cor 13), would say, "Put them on."

Saying No to Friendship with the World

James writes again in 4:1–4 about the inner motivations that pressure us to serve ourselves. Twice he uses the word *hēdonē*, which stands for passion, lust, or pleasure, and from which we get the word "hedonistic." Craving and coveting (v. 2) lead to violent outcomes when there is concern only about oneself. These tendencies toward self-gratification are interpreted theologically in 4:4–10. They are indications of a very basic dysfunction in relationship with God. Writing now as a prophet, James thunders out the Old Testament image of adultery as breaking the covenant that God has made with his people. For example, Ezek 16 describes in great detail how Israel has been unfaithful. The Lord had appointed her as his bride, but by going after idols and other gods she became like a prostitute. God is extremely angry: "You adulterous wife! You prefer strangers to your own husband!" (Ezek 16:32). Adulterers are more interested in satisfying their selfish desires than in being faithful to their promises and commitments, so James is challenging his readers to refresh their relationship to God and to maintain it faithfully. They need to say *no* to their self-serving interests and attend to God.

James immediately presents the problem in another way—to maintain a "friendship with the world" is in reality to be an enemy of God! By this he certainly does not mean that we should try to escape from the normal business of living in the world of family and society. John's first letter explains this: "All that is in the world, the lust of the flesh and the lust of the eyes and the pride of life, is not of the Father but is of the world" (1 John 2:15–17). "Friendship with the world" is accepting and adopting the norms and values of a culture that does not acknowledge God. It is seeing things from a perspective that takes no account of God. It is living by a system of values that leaves God out of the picture. It is ignoring God, forgetting God. Friendship with the world feeds on a drive for self-determination and the power of natural unredeemed passions. It is not the way to follow Christ.

The alternative is friendship with God, the one source of life and wisdom. This is not the kind of friendship that is just affection, or nice feelings for one another, or acquaintance on Facebook. In first-century society, to be a friend (*philos*) was to share the same attitudes and values and perceptions, to see things the same way, to agree with one another, even to share material possessions. It was equality on many levels. Abraham is described as a "friend of God" in 2:23. This means, according to the ancient definition of friendship, that Abraham accepted God's way of seeing things. If he had been a friend of "the world" he would not have obeyed God when God asked him to sacrifice his only son Isaac. To be a friend of God is to accept God's system of values, and to see things from God's perspective. It is to agree with God.

This decision—whether to be a friend of God or a friend of the world—is not a once-for-all decision. It needs to be renewed continually, because, as James says, "we all stumble in many ways" (3:2). There is an internal battle (4:1). Paul writes in a similar way in Gal 5:16–18. The struggle needs to be kept active, in order to live a devout and holy life.[6]

Denying Selfish Ambition

James gives a specific example of selfish ambition in 4:13–16. The imaginary readers assume that it is appropriate to leave God out of their plans. James is not criticizing the drive to do business and make money and compete for clients, for these are normal activities of living. The problem is again self-centeredness and the desire for personal gain. Self-centered boasting

---

6. See further Johnson, "Friendship With the World," 166–83.

assumes that we are in control, but in reality, all our plans are subject to the will of God. James then gives his answer to these people (4:14). First he emphasizes human ignorance—we cannot predict the future, so all our plans must be provisional (cf. Prov 27:1). We must relinquish our own will in planning independently of God. Then he asks a rhetorical question, "What is your life?" (4:14), challenging his readers to focus on the fragile nature of life and the purpose of their existence. Such reflection should be an antidote to arrogance and selfish ambition.

1 PETER

Peter's first letter encourages personal transformation through the realization of new identity and the practice of discipline. 1 Pet 1:13–16 gives a series of imperatives that serve as exhortations to live a disciplined and holy life. Peter writes, "Therefore prepare your minds for action; discipline yourselves; set all your hope on the grace that Jesus Christ will bring you when he is revealed." The word "therefore" is important, because it looks back to the narrative of salvation that Peter has reminded his readers of in the preceding verses. On this basis Peter appeals for a response to the salvation that God has provided.

A Call to Self-Discipline

"Prepare your minds for action" (1:13) appropriately interprets the Greek imperative that says, literally, "Gird up the loins of your mind." Tucking up one's garments with a belt was, in biblical times, a necessary preparation for physical activity, so that the clothing would not get in the way. Here the metaphor is a summons to a vigorous commitment to the Christian life. It begins with the mind, which must be got ready; we must take control of our thoughts, putting aside what is harmful or not helpful, especially the "evil desires" that are mentioned in verse 14. "Discipline yourselves" translates the Greek word for "be sober" (*nēphō*). This imperative is repeated in 4:7 and 5:8, where it is linked to alertness and sensible thinking. To be sober, in the literal sense, is to say *no* to intoxication and drunkenness, and this is what Peter may mean (cf. 4:3–4), a command expressed more explicitly in Eph 5:18. But "being sober" also refers to self-control in other areas—having a well-balanced perspective and a clear mind, free of fuzziness.[7] In Peter's Greek text the word for "completely" is sandwiched between the words for "sober" and "hope," and it is not entirely clear whether we are to understand "completely sober" or "fix your hope completely."[8] A commitment to "set all one's hope" on the grace of Christ is based not only on what God has already done for believers, but also on what God will do in the future. Here again we find honor language together with eschatological language; both motivate Christian endeavor, for God's grace (his unmerited favor toward us) will be fully revealed when Christ comes again.

"Like obedient children, do not be conformed to the desires that you formerly had" (1:14). Peter here uses a word that is used also by Paul in Rom 12:2—"Don't be *conformed* to this world but be *transformed* by the renewing of your minds." Though Peter refers here only to the "desires" (which we should understand as evil desires, as in 4:3) the thought is the same as Paul's. Followers of Jesus have adopted a new theocentric world-view that includes the realization that they are children of God, and so, in order to align themselves with the character and intentions of the Father, they must make adjustments to their thinking and behavior, and they must say *no* to things that were previously acceptable to them.

"Be holy in all your conduct" (1:15). For the word "conduct" (*anastrophē*) we could use today's term "lifestyle."[9] Here is the idea of separation from "the world." Instead of being conformed to the distorted ways of the dominant culture (the "futile way of life inherited from ancestors" in 1:18), Christians are to conform themselves to the character of God, and live in ways that are appropriate for God's children. Peter expects a high standard of conduct that will set believers apart from the lifestyles of the wider society. He does not prescribe specific practices of self-denial or asceticism, but presents general principles of personal attitudes and exemplary behavior, founded firmly on the theological basis of new identity in Christ.

---

7. Paul writes in 2 Tim 4:5, "Be sober in all things," and in 1 Thess 5:6 urges alertness to spiritual realities: "Let us keep awake and be sober."

8. McKnight (*1 Peter*) gives a strong argument for "totally self-controlled" based on Peter's preference for certain adverbs to follow their verbs.

9. *Anastrophē* is used six times in this letter, and can be translated as conduct, behavior, way of life. Peter's concern for good, pure Christian conduct in the public sphere is very evident (see 2:12; 3:1, 2, 16).

Following in Jesus' Steps

Several times in this letter Peter refers to the sufferings of Christ (1:11; 2:21; 3:18; 4:1, 13; 5:1). In 2:18–21 he links the sufferings of Christian slaves with the suffering that Jesus experienced. Jesus is the example who shows us how to respond to unmerited suffering. The word for "example" is *hypogrammos*, which refers to the written pattern over which children were taught to trace the letters of the alphabet. Jesus, then, left this pattern over which his followers are to trace out their lives.[10] This implies that Christians should expect to be treated unjustly—it will be no surprise if people mock us or despise us or cause us to suffer. Peter provides here a vivid commentary on Jesus' words in the "self-denial" saying, explaining what it means to "take up the cross" (Mark 8:34). He clearly expects Jesus' disciples to "follow in his steps" (2:21) so that they "share his sufferings" (4:13). Here we must acknowledge the existential challenges that the word "cross" evokes. "Taking up the cross" brings us face-to-face with pain and suffering of many kinds. Following Jesus, then, is difficult. But Peter, like Jesus in the Gospels, reminds us that faithful, patient endurance of unmerited suffering is an honorable activity, commendable in the sight of God. It is "to your credit" (*charis*, v. 19) and brings "God's approval" (*charis* again in v. 20).

Redefining Suffering and Shame

Chapters 3 and 4 of the letter continue to use honor language, as they speak of the suffering of persecution and the kinds of behavior that are appropriate for Christ's followers. A pair of parallel statements appears in 3:14. The first says, "Even if you suffer for righteousness' sake, you are blessed (*makarios*)." Even more explicit is 4:14, which says, "If you are insulted for the name of Christ, you are blessed, because the Spirit of glory, who is the Spirit of God, rests on you." Peter is redefining the dishonor of human persecution as honor given by God. The second statement in 3:14 makes a similar contrast: "Have no fear of them . . . but reverence Christ as Lord." We may hear in this statement an echo of Jesus' words in Matt 10:28, "Do not fear those who kill the body." Fear of what people can do may often betray a misguided tendency to elevate their power, importance, and significance, and to forget that God is more powerful, more important, and more significant. This kind of fear, then, is another thing to say *no* to.

10. Jobes, *1 Peter*, 195.

In 4:1–2 Peter again draws attention to the example of the suffering Christ. He urges his readers to have "the same intention" (*ennoia*). By this he may mean the same attitude as Jesus, who in his suffering submitted to God's will (cf. 2:23) rather than to his own human desires. Alternatively, *ennoia* may refer to the understanding that, as Christ through his suffering is now finished with sin, we also are to have no dealings with sin.[11] It is better to suffer than to sin. Giving in to temptation is often based on unwillingness to suffer the consequences of telling the truth, to suffer loss of reputation, or to suffer the pain of unfulfilled emotional and physical needs and desires. But it is necessary for followers of Jesus to embrace suffering.

What motivation does Peter provide for saying *no* to unhealthy desires and to the ways of the world, and for being willing to deny oneself and "take up the cross"? Peter's strong imperatives are founded on an abundance of equally solid indicatives. Special emphasis is given to the new identity of Christ-followers, whom God has called his children (1:14, 17) and on whom God has bestowed much honor (1:13; 2:4, 19, 20). As well, there is the prospect of eschatological blessing at Christ's coming (1:7, 13; 4:13; 5:1, 10). For these reasons, and because believers are called to holiness (1:15, 16) Christians will strive to follow Jesus; this implies personal transformation through discipline. Peter writes near the end of his letter, "Humble yourselves therefore under the mighty hand of God, so that he may exalt you in due time" (5:6). This expresses well the attitude that is required for Christian self-denial, which is authentic only as it relates in trust and submission to God.

JUDE

When Self-Denial Doesn't Happen

The letters of Jude and 2 Peter illustrate the lack of self-control exhibited by certain false teachers. Jude describes certain charlatans who are certainly into denial—the trouble is that they deny the Master, Jesus Christ, rather than themselves (v. 4). Jude describes them as self-indulgent and libertine. They "care for themselves" (v. 12), "indulge their own lusts," and are concerned only for their own advantage (v. 16). They are "worldly" (*psychikoi*) and devoid of the Spirit (v. 19). They stand, therefore, at the opposite pole

---

11. Richard, *Reading*, 168.

from the New Testament's depiction of those who deny themselves for the sake of Christ.

2 PETER

"Making Every Effort"

The second letter of Peter appears to be a later epistle that is to a large extent an expansion of Jude's. It says similar things about false prophets who "secretly bring in destructive opinions" (2:1). These bad examples show no self-control—instead they are slanderous (2:10–12) and greedy (2:3, 14), giving expression to their corrupt desires (2:10; 3:3). To counter these distortions, the writer urges in 1:5–7 a striving for goodness, knowledge, self-control, endurance, godliness, mutual affection, and love. Although these virtues are conventional ones, the author views them in a distinctively Christian light, for they are necessary for effective and fruitful following of Christ (1:8) and their presence in the believers is a result of the cleansing of their past sins (1:9). The reason for these imperatives is given in the preceding verses (1:3–4), which describe three ways in which God has blessed believers. First, he has provided, through his divine power, "everything needed for life and godliness" so that, while we must strive to live a disciplined life of self-denial (3:14), we already have the resources to do so, and need not be dependent on our own strength. Second, he has "called us to his own glory and excellence" (ESV).[12] This is an invitation to share the glory of God—a status of the highest honor—echoing Paul's thought in 2 Cor 3:18 ("being transformed into the same image [the glory of the Lord] from one degree of glory to another"). Third, he has given us great promises, through which (by believing them and acting on them) we are able to "escape from the corruption that is in the world because of lust, and may become participants in the divine nature" (1:4). This "divine nature" is probably best seen, not as a reference to God's essential being, but as a contrast to the earthly nature of present existence—its temporality and impurity. That is, though we live in a morally polluted world, we have the sure hope of becoming fully realized citizens of the kingdom of God, in which we enjoy eternal life. So, for all of these reasons, we are to "make every effort" (1:10; 3:14 NIV) to discipline ourselves so that we are effective and productive (1:8) as followers of Jesus.

---

12. The reading "to" instead of "through" is attested by a broad spectrum of manuscripts (see Metzger, *Textual Commentary*).

There is a strong eschatological perspective in 3:10–13. The "day of the Lord" will arrive suddenly, and this reminder prompts the author to ask a rhetorical question that requires of his readers some self-reflection: while they are waiting expectantly for Christ's coming, "What sort of people ought you to be?" (3:11). He actually helps to answer the question, for he adds, "in leading lives of holiness and godliness," but he notes also that this will require diligence and effort (3:14).

JOHN'S LETTERS

Laying Down Our Lives

The only verse in 1 John that refers specifically to self-denial is 3:16—"We know love by this, that he laid down his life for us, and we ought to lay down our lives for one another." This relates, of course, to Jesus' sayings about "losing one's life" (Mark 8:35) and "giving his life" (Mark 10:45; John 10:15–18; 15:13). John's use of the verb *opheilein* ("ought") here and in 4:11 emphasizes that this willingness to donate oneself for another's benefit— whether in large ways or small—is an obligation for those who have benefited from Jesus' sacrifice. It is an expression of the love that John writes so much about (1 John 4:7–21), and which is the ultimate motivation for self-denial. These pastoral letters repeat again and again the mutuality of relationships within the fellowship of believers—the attitude that relativizes self-interest. John writes six times, "Love one another" (1 John 3:11, 23; 4:7, 11, 12; 2 John 5). This emphasis is strengthened by the way John addresses his readers many times—as a*gapētoi*, beloved (2:7; 3:2, 21; 4:1, 7, 11; 3 John 1, 2, 5, 11). This word conveys not only John's own attachment to his readers, but also, and perhaps primarily, the Father's own love for them as children of God. Like Peter and Paul, John is eager for his people to grasp the wonder of their new identity as those who have been cleansed from sin (1:7), anointed by the Spirit (2:20; 3:24; 4:13), accepted as God's children (3:1–2; 5:19), and given eternal life (5:11). These are tokens of highest honor.

John, like James, knows that love expressed in mere words is inadequate without accompanying action. "How does God's love abide in anyone who has the world's goods and sees a brother or sister in need and yet refuses help?" (1 John 3:17). This rhetorical question is an implicit exhortation for John's readers to divest themselves of their own resources and security for the sake of others.

Walking in the Light

John writes that followers of Jesus must "walk in the light" (1 John 1:7) and "walk in the truth" (2 John 4). The verb "walk" (*peripatein*) is used seventeen times in the Fourth Gospel and ten times in John's letters. Most of these occurrences use "walking" as a metaphor for one's conduct or manner of life.[13] According to 1 John 2:6, Christians have an obligation "to walk just as he walked." Here John refers to Jesus' way of life in the years of his ministry on earth. The inference, like that of 1 Pet 2:21, is that we should "follow in his steps," taking him as the example. John's letters do not use the language of "following Jesus" (*akolouthein*) that we find in Jesus' self-denial saying, but John's Gospel puts the two verbs in parallel: Jesus says, "Whoever *follows* me will never *walk* in darkness" (John 8:12). John's letters, then, add content to what it means to follow Jesus.

A Bad Example

The third letter of John presents us with an example of a leader who apparently did not understand or practice self-denial. It is Diotrephes, "who likes to put himself first" (3 John 9), not accepting John's authority and apparently wielding his own power in ways that are incompatible with walking in truth and love. In contrast with Diotrephes are John's visitors—fellow-workers who "went out for the sake of the Name" that is, the name of Jesus (v. 7).

REVELATION

The book of Revelation is an encouragement for first-century followers of Jesus, who were facing hostility and persecution from the dominant Roman culture because of their faith in Christ. Using language that is highly symbolic, it uncovers what could not be seen without spiritual vision: amid trouble and conflict, God is still in control; Christ is Lord and will eventually

---

13. This metaphor, originally expressed in Hebrew by *halak* (e.g., Ps 1:1), is often used by Paul (e.g., Gal 5:16).

conquer the enemies of God's people. Believers are to endure their trials and bear faithful witness, in the sure hope that they will participate in the victory. In this context, the book affirms the honor of those Christians who have not denied their faith in Christ (2:13)—those who have kept his word and not denied his name (3:8).

Saying No to Idolatry

There is an implication of self-denial in 14:4, which speaks of the 144,000 "who have not defiled themselves with women, for they are virgins." Does this refer to a special category of Christians who have renounced marriage? No, for a couple of reasons. First, the number 144,000 is figurative, as are all the numbers in this book; it denotes the totality of God's redeemed people throughout the ages.[14] They are singing praises to God for the victory he has won for them over their enemies. Second, it follows that the reference to "virgins" is also figurative, as is the metaphor of the bride of Christ (19:7–9 and 21:2) and the metaphor of the harlot Babylon (14:8). Therefore, the passage refers not to any renunciation of sexual activity, but to refusal to participate in the idolatrous practices of Roman imperial society.

Following the Lamb

Also in 14:4 we read that these redeemed believers "follow the Lamb wherever he goes." There is an obvious allusion here to Gospel texts like Mark 8:34, in which Jesus invites people to follow him, and especially Luke 9:57–58 (= Matt 8:19–20), where a would-be disciple says, "I will follow you wherever you go."[15] These believers have transferred their allegiance from the world to Christ; they have imitated his faithfulness in the midst of suffering and persecution. Some of them have followed him to death as martyrs (6:9; 12:11). We hear an echo of the "losing life" saying (Mark 8:35) in 12:11—"they did not cling to life even in the face of death."

The only reference to the cross in Revelation is in 11:8. It occurs within a graphic description of the death of the two faithful witnesses (11:3) who

14. Beale, *Book of Revelation*, 733.

15. Aune ("Following the Lamb," 275) says that this phrase from the Q material probably indicates "the early existence of a very simple, yet potentially profound, generic conception of discipleship." See also Longenecker's Introduction, an overview of discipleship language, in the same volume, 1–5.

give public testimony in God's name. They are killed by their enemies and their bodies are left shamefully in the street of the "great city." They have suffered the same fate as Christ—they have "taken up their cross" and followed him to death. It is reasonable to view the two witnesses as representing the total body of redeemed believers, in which case this passage depicts the decline of the church in the final days of this world.[16] But the good news is announced without delay: like the dry bones in the valley of Ezek 37, they receive the breath of God and are raised up to heaven. This revelation declares that although faithful discipleship brings shame in the eyes of the world, the faithful are ultimately honored by God: "those who lose their life for my sake, and for the sake of the gospel, will save it" (Mark 8:35).

---

16. Beale, *Book of Revelation*, 573–76.

CHAPTER 5

Summary

Having surveyed the entire New Testament, we can now take a broad, though brief, view of what we have found. The Synoptic Gospels provided the starting-point for our examination of self-denial, because they are the only texts that contain the words of Jesus, "If any want to become my followers, let them deny themselves and take up their cross and follow me." The meaning of this saying, and those sayings associated with it, is unfolded and expanded by many other teachings of Jesus in all four Gospels. We found that a necessary element in the interpretation of the self-denial concept was the very significant emphasis on considerations of honor and shame in the first-century culture in which Jesus and his disciples lived. Self-denial, for Jesus, would require a radical renunciation of one's claims on wealth, family, social status, and even one's own life. In responding to Jesus' claims, and in committing themselves to follow him, disciples would have to give priority to their attachment to him, and to God the Father, which would mean revaluing their attachment to everything else: home, family, economic security, status, plans, and ambitions. They would have to reorient their worldview away from the "self" as center and toward God, on the basis of the surpassing worth of the honor God had ascribed to them.

We then discovered in the letters of Paul and his associates many passages that are congruent with the perspective of the Gospels. Paul's teaching is based on his recognition of the supremacy of Jesus Christ and the transformed identity he received through the Holy Spirit. This transformation, foreshadowed in the Gospels ("you must be born again . . . you must become like children") entails a reorientation of both mind and heart, that must be made evident in changed attitudes and behavior. Therefore, Paul insists that believers must think of themselves in a way that differentiates between the "old" and the "new." They must embrace a realistic perception of themselves as people loved, honored, and nurtured by God. With this perspective, they will be motivated to forsake the sins and temptations of the world, the "flesh" and the devil, and to practice self-control regarding the passions inherent in their human nature. Since this is not an easy task, Paul encourages believers to work hard to govern, discipline, and train themselves to think and act in ways that honor God.

But Paul insists not only on the rejection of immorality and other vices, but also on the necessity for followers of Jesus to relegate personal interests (even their good, legitimate concerns and rights) to a lower place, in order to focus on serving others and nurturing them in the Christian faith. This is a close reflection of the kind of self-denial required by Jesus in the Gospels. Paul's instructions in this regard are based on the same foundations: honor granted by God, love for one another, eschatological hope, and imitation of Christ. This attitude of self-denial will be demonstrated in relinquishing one's freedom for the benefit of others and for the progress of the gospel. Followers of Jesus who are "denying themselves" will not boast of status and worldly honors. They will be willing to suffer for others. They will even lay down their lives for others. Paul's letters give testimony to his commitment to this project. As he imitates Jesus, Paul himself is an example to his readers.

The Pauline letters also point out, however, that self-denial can be taken to an inappropriate extreme. Self-denial is not the rejection or negation of one's self, or the debasing of one's personality. Nor does the practice of godly self-discipline require any unwarranted abstinence from food, marriage, or social interaction in the world.

The non-Pauline epistles are consistently in agreement with the perspectives of Paul and the Gospel writers. The author of Hebrews legitimates the faithful following of Jesus by invalidating the system of honor operated by his first-century society, and encourages followers toward self-discipline and the renunciation of hindrances to discipleship. James concentrates on the importance of saying *no* to the pollutions of the world, urging a realistic apprehension of our human nature, especially in regard to self-focus and the use of the tongue. Peter, building on the foundation of the believer's God-given identity, exhorts us to self-discipline and a holy life as we follow in Jesus' steps, despite the suffering and shame that such self-denial may bring. For John, love for one another is the controlling motivation to "walk in the light" and reject dark ways. The book of Revelation draws specific attention to the need to say *no* to idolatry, and encourages believers to persevere in the midst of the suffering that may be a result of adhering to Christian belief.

On the whole, the New Testament presents Christian believers with a substantial challenge. It speaks of radical transformation of values, attitudes, and behaviors. These transformations are evidence of the abundant life of God's reign that Jesus came to give (John 10:10). They force us to think deeply about our identity, our motivations, and our relationships. They are foundational for how we think about self-denial, and for how we practice it if we desire to follow Christ in the twenty-first century.

Bibliography

Albright, W. F. *Matthew*. Anchor Bible. New Haven, CT: Yale University Press, 1995.

Aune, David E. "Following the Lamb: Discipleship in the Apocalypse." In *Patterns of Discipleship in the NT*, edited by R. Longenecker, 269–84. Grand Rapids: Eerdmans, 1996.

Bailey, Kenneth E. *Through Peasant Eyes*. Combined edition with *Poet and Peasant: A Literary-Cultural Approach to the Parables in Luke*. Grand Rapids: Eerdmans, 1983.

Balch, David L. "Rich and Poor, Proud and Humble in Luke-Acts." In *The Social World of the First Christians: Essays in Honor of Wayne A. Meeks*, edited by L. Michael White and O. Larry Yarbrough, 214–33. Minneapolis: Fortress, 1995.

Barnett, Paul. *The Second Epistle to the Corinthians*. Grand Rapids: Eerdmans, 1997.

Barr, Steve. "The Eye of the Needle—Power and Money in the New Community: A Look at Mark 10:17–31." *Andover Newton Review* 3 (1992) 31–44.

Barton, Stephen C. *Discipleship and Family Ties in Mark and Matthew*. Cambridge: Cambridge University Press, 1994.

————. "The Relativisation of Family Ties in the Jewish and Greco-Roman Traditions." In *Constructing Early Christian Families: Family as Social Reality and Metaphor*, edited by Halvor Moxnes, 81–100. London: Routledge, 1997.

Beale, Gregory K. *The Book of Revelation*. NIGTC. Grand Rapids: Eerdmans, 1999.

Bird, Michael F. *An Anomalous Jew: Paul among Jews, Greeks, and Romans*. Grand Rapids: Eerdmans, 2016.

Bultmann, Rudolf. *Theology of the NT*. Vol. 1. London: SCM, 1952.

Burridge, Richard A. *Imitating Jesus: An Inclusive Approach to New Testament Ethics*. Grand Rapids: Eerdmans, 2007.

Byrne, Brendan. *Romans*. Sacra Pagina 6. Collegeville, MN: Liturgical, 1996.

Caba, José. "From Lukan Parenesis to Johannine Christology: Luke 9:23–24 and John 12:25–26." In *Luke and Acts*, edited by Gerald O'Collins and Gilberto Marconi, 48–71. Mahwah, NJ: Paulist, 1993.

Castelli, Elizabeth A. *Imitating Paul: A Discourse of Power*. Louisville, KY: Westminster John Knox, 1991.

Christensen, Sean M. "The Pursuit of Self-Control: Titus 2:1–14 and Accommodation to Christ." *Journal for the Study of Paul and His Letters* 6.2 (2016) 161–80.

Cranfield, Charles E. B. "Self-Denial." *Expository Times* 104/5 (1993) 143–45.

Croy, N. Clayton. *Endurance in Suffering*. Cambridge: Cambridge University Press, 1998.

Danylak, Barry. *Redeeming Singleness: How the Storyline of Scripture Affirms the Single Life*. Wheaton, IL: Crossway, 2010.

BIBLIOGRAPHY

deSilva, David A. *Bearing Christ's Reproach: The Challenge of Hebrews in an Honor Culture*. North Richland Hills, TX: BIBAL, 1999.

———. "Despising Shame: A Cultural-Anthropological Investigation of the Epistle to the Hebrews." *Journal of Biblical Literature* 113 (1994) 439–61.

———. *Despising Shame: Honor Discourse and Community Maintenance in the Epistle to the Hebrews*. Rev. ed. Atlanta: SBL, 2008.

———. *The Hope of Glory: Honor Discourse and NT Interpretation*. Collegeville, MN: Liturgical, 1999.

Donaldson, Terence L. *Paul and the Gentiles: Remapping the Apostle's Convictional World*. Minneapolis: Fortress, 1997.

Downing, F. Gerald. "'Honor' among Exegetes." *Catholic Biblical Quarterly* 61 (1999) 53–73.

Dunn, James D. G. *Jesus, Paul, and the Gospels*. Grand Rapids: Eerdmans, 2011.

———. *Romans 1–8*. Word Biblical Commentary. Waco, TX: Word, 1988.

Dürr, Simon. "'Your Fully Human Vocation': The Meaning of the *logike latreia hymon* (Rom 12:1c) Reconsidered." SBL International Meeting Abstract, August 2017.

Engberg-Pedersen, Troels. "Complete and Incomplete Transformation in Paul: A Philosophical Reading of Paul on Body and Spirit." In *Metamorphoses: Resurrection, Body and Transformative Practices in Early Christianity*, edited by Turid Karlsen Seim and Jorunn Økland, 123–46. Berlin: Walter de Gruyter, 2009.

———. "Radical Altruism in Philippians 2:4." In *Early Christianity and Classical Culture*, edited by John T. Fitzgerald et al., 197–214. Leiden: Brill, 2003.

Evans, Craig A. *Mark 8:27—16:20*. Word Biblical Commentary 34B. Nashville: Thomas Nelson, 2001.

Fee, Gordon D. *The First Epistle to the Corinthians*. Rev. ed. NICNT. Grand Rapids: Eerdmans, 2014.

———. *Galatians*. Pentecostal Commentary Series. Blandford Forum: Deo, 2007.

———. *Paul's Letter to the Philippians*. NICNT. Grand Rapids: Eerdmans, 1995.

———. "Philippians 2:5–11: Hymn or Exalted Pauline Prose?" *Bulletin for Biblical Research* 2 (1992) 29–46.

Ferguson, Everett. *Backgrounds of Early Christianity*. 2nd ed. Grand Rapids: Eerdmans, 1993.

Fletcher, Donald R. "Condemned to Die: The Logion on Cross-bearing—What Does it Mean?" *Interpretation* 18 (1964) 162.

Fowl, Stephen E. *Ephesians: A Commentary*. Louisville, KY: Westminster John Knox, 2012.

Francis, James. *Adults as Children: Images of Childhood in the Ancient World and the New Testament*. Bern: Peter Lang, 2006.

———. "Children and Childhood in the New Testament." In *The Family in Theological Perspective*, edited by S. C. Barton, 66–72. Edinburgh: T. & T. Clark, 1994.

Fung, Ronald Y. K. *The Epistle to the Galatians*. NICNT. Grand Rapids: Eerdmans, 1988.

Garland, David E. *1 Corinthians*. Baker Exegetical Commentary. Grand Rapids: Baker Academic, 2003.

Garrett, Susan R. "Beloved Physician of the Soul? Luke as Advocate for Ascetic Practice." In *Asceticism and the NT*, edited by Leif E. Vaage and Vincent L. Wimbush, 71–95. New York: Routledge, 1999.

Gay, Craig. *The Way of the (Modern) World: Or, Why It's Tempting to Live as if God Doesn't Exist*. Grand Rapids: Eerdmans, 1998.

Green, Joel. *Gospel of Luke*. Grand Rapids: Eerdmans, 1997.

Bibliography

Griffith-Jones, Robin. "'Keep Up Your Transformation within the Renewal of Your Mind': Romans as a Therapeutic Letter." In *Experientia*, Vol. 2, *Linking Text and Experience*, edited by Colleen Shantz and Rodney A. Werline, 137–60. Atlanta: SBL, 2012.

Griffiths, J. Gwyn. "The Disciple's Cross." *New Testament Studies* 16 (1970) 358–64.

Gupta, Nijay K. *Colossians*. Smyth & Helwys Bible Commentary. Macon, GA: Smyth & Helwys, 2013.

Hafemann, Scott J. *2 Corinthians*. NIV Application Commentary. Grand Rapids: Zondervan, 2000.

———. "Self-Commendation and Apostolic Legitimacy in 2 Corinthians: A Pauline Dialectic?" *New Testament Studies* 36 (1990) 66–88.

Hanson, K. C. "How Honorable! How Shameful! A Cultural Analysis of Matthew's Makarisms and Reproaches." *Semeia* 68 (1994) 81–111.

Hellerman, Joseph H. *The Ancient Church as Family*. Minneapolis: Fortress, 2001.

Hengel, Martin. *The Charismatic Leader and His Followers*. Edinburgh: T. & T. Clark, 1981.

Hock, Ronald F. "God's Will at Thessalonica and Greco-Roman Asceticism." In *Asceticism and the New Testament*, edited by Leif E. Vaage and Vincent L. Wimbush, 159–70. New York: Routledge, 1999.

Holmberg, Bengt. *Sociology and the New Testament: An Appraisal*. Minneapolis: Fortress, 1990.

Jewett, Robert. *Romans: A Commentary*. Hermeneia. Minneapolis: Fortress, 2007.

Jobes, Karen H. *1 Peter*. Baker Exegetical Commentary on the New Testament. Grand Rapids: Baker Academic, 2015.

Johnson, Luke T. *The First and Second Letters to Timothy*. Anchor Bible. New York: Doubleday, 2001.

———. "Friendship With the World/Friendship with God: A Study of Discipleship in James." In *Discipleship in the New Testament*, edited by F. F. Segovia, 166–83. Philadelphia: Fortress, 1985.

———. *The Gospel of Luke*. Sacra Pagina. Collegeville, MN: Liturgical, 1991.

Kaelber, Walter O. "Asceticism." In *The Encyclopedia of Religion*, vol. 1., edited by Mircea Eliade, 441–45. New York: Macmillan, 1987.

Keener, Craig S. *The Mind of the Spirit: Paul's Approach to Transformed Thinking*. Grand Rapids: Baker Academic, 2016.

Koch, Robert. "Self-Denial." In *Encyclopedia of Biblical Theology: The Complete Sacramentum Verbi*, edited by Johannes B. Bauer, 833–39. New York: Crossroad, 1981.

Lane, William L. *The Gospel According to Mark*. Grand Rapids: Eerdmans, 1974.

Lasch, Christopher. *The Culture of Narcissism*. New York: Norton, 1979.

———. *The Minimal Self*. New York: Norton, 1985.

Lee, Jae Hyun. "'Think' and 'Do' like the Role Models: Paul's Teaching on the Christian Life in Philippians." In *The Language and Literature of the New Testament*, edited by Lois K. Fuller Dow, Craig A. Evans, and Andrew W. Pitts, 625–43. Leiden: Brill, 2017.

Lindars, Barnabas. *The Gospel of John*. New Century Bible. London: Oliphants, 1972.

Lipset, S. M. "Social Class." *International Encyclopedia of the Social Sciences* 15 (1968) 296–316.

Lynch, Ted. "Transcending Desire: The Shaping of Christian Thought by Classical Ideals of Restraint and Transcendence." PhD dissertation, North-West University, 2016.

MacDonald, Margaret Y. "Citizens of Heaven and Earth: Asceticism and Social Integration in Colossians and Ephesians." In *Asceticism and the New Testament*, edited by Leif E. Vaage and Vincent L. Wimbush, 269–98. New York: Routledge, 1999.

———. *Colossians and Ephesians*. Sacra Pagina. Collegeville, MN: Liturgical, 2000.

Malina, Bruce. "'Let Him Deny Himself' (Mark 8:34 & Par): A Social Psychological Model of Self-Denial." *Biblical Theology Bulletin* 24 (1994) 106–19.

———. "Pain, Power and Personhood: Ascetic Behavior in the Ancient Mediterranean." In *Asceticism*, edited by Vincent L. Wimbush and Richard Valantasis, 162–77. New York: Oxford University Press, 1995.

———. "Patron and Client: The Analogy Behind Synoptic Theology." *Forum* 4 (1988) 2–32.

Malina, Bruce, and Richard L. Rohrbaugh. *Social-Science Commentary on the Gospel of John*. Minneapolis: Fortress, 1998.

Manne, Anne. *The Life of I: The New Culture of Narcissism*. Melbourne: Melbourne University Press, 2014.

Maslow, Abraham. *Motivation and Personality*. New York: Harper, 1954.

May, David M. "Leaving and Receiving: A Social-Scientific Exegesis of Mark 10:29–31." *Perspectives in Religious Studies* 17 (1990) 141–54.

Mayes, A. D. H. *Deuteronomy*. New Century Bible Commentary. Grand Rapids: Eerdmans, 1981.

McKnight, Scot. *1 Peter*. Grand Rapids: Zondervan, 1996.

Meeks, Wayne A. "The Social Level of Pauline Christians." In *Social-Scientific Approaches to New Testament Interpretation*, edited by David G. Horrell, 195–232. Edinburgh: T. & T. Clark, 1999.

Metzger, B. M. *Textual Commentary on the Greek New Testament*. 2nd ed. Stuttgart: Deutsche Bibelgesellschaft, 1994.

Michel, O. "*Miseō*." In *Theological Dictionary of the New Testament*, vol. 4, edited by Gerhard Kittel, 683–94. Grand Rapids: Eerdmans, 1987.

Milbank, John. "The Ethics of Self-Sacrifice." *First Things*, March 1999. https://www.firstthings.com/article/1999/03/004-the-ethics-of-self-sacrifice.

Moeser, Marion C. *The Anecdote in Mark, the Classical World and the Rabbis*. Sheffield: Sheffield Academic, 2002.

Mohrlang, Roger, and Gerald L. Borchert. *Romans and Galatians*. Cornerstone Biblical Commentary 14. Carol Stream, IL: Tyndale, 2007.

Neufeld, Dietmar, and Richard E. DeMaris, eds. *Understanding the Social World of the New Testament*. New York: Routledge, 2010.

Neyrey, Jerome H. "Despising the Shame of the Cross: Honor and Shame in the Johannine Passion Narrative." *Semeia* 68 (1994) 113–37.

———. *Honor and Shame in the Gospel of Matthew*. Louisville, KY: Westminster John Knox, 1998.

———. "Loss of Wealth, Loss of Family and Loss of Honor: The Cultural Context of the Original Makarisms in Q." In *Modelling Early Christianity*, edited by Philip F. Esler, 139–58. London: Routledge, 1995.

Neyrey, Jerome H., and Eric C. Stewart, eds. *The Social World of the New Testament*. Peabody, MA: Hendrickson, 2008.

Nolland, John. *Luke 9:21—18:34*. Word Biblical Commentary 35B. Dallas: Word, 1993.

Oakes, Peter. *Reading Romans in Pompeii: Paul's Letter at Ground Level*. London: SPCK, 2009.

BIBLIOGRAPHY

Packer, James I. "The 'Wretched Man' Revisited: Another Look at Romans 7:14–25." In *Romans and the People of God*, edited by S. K. Soderlund and N. T. Wright, 70–81. Grand Rapids: Eerdmans, 1999.

Pawlak, Matthew C. "Consistency Isn't Everything: Self-Commendation in 2 Corinthians." *Journal for the Study of the New Testament* 40 (2018) 360–82.

Plutarch. *On Praising Oneself Inoffensively*. Loeb Classical Library 405. Cambridge: Harvard University Press, 1959.

Porter, Stanley E. *The Letter to the Romans: A Linguistic and Literary Commentary.* Sheffield: Sheffield Phoenix, 2015.

Rensberger, David. "Asceticism and the Gospel of John." In *Asceticism and the New Testament*, edited by Leif E. Vaage and Vincent L. Wimbush, 127–47. New York: Routledge, 1999.

Richard, Earl J. *Reading 1 Peter, Jude, and 2 Peter.* Macon, GA: Smyth & Helwys, 2000.

Richter, Philip. "Social-Scientific Criticism of the NT: An Appraisal and Extended Example." In *Approaches to NT Study*, edited by Stanley E. Porter and David Tombs, 266–309. Sheffield: Sheffield Academic, 1995.

Rochester, Stuart T. "Honor as a Foundation for Self-Denial in the Synoptic Gospels." https://www.academia.edu/18485419/Honour_as_a_Foundation_for_Self-denial_in_the_Synoptic_Gospels_revised_Nov_2015.

Schlier, Heinrich. *"Arneomai."* In *Theological Dictionary of the New Testament*, vol. 1, edited by Gerhard Kittel, 469–71. Grand Rapids: Eerdmans, 1987.

Schoberg, Gerry. *Perspectives of Jesus in the Writings of Paul: A Historical Examination of Shared Core Commitments with a View to Determining the Extent of Paul's Dependence on Jesus.* Eugene, OR: Pickwick, 2013.

Seccombe, David P. "Take Up Your Cross." In *God Who Is Rich in Mercy: Essays Presented to Dr D.B. Knox*, edited by P. T. O'Brien and D. G. Peterson, 139–51. Homebush, NSW: Lancer, 1986.

Seifrid, Mark A. *The Second Letter to the Corinthians.* Grand Rapids: Eerdmans, 2014.

Smit, Peter-Ben. "Paul, Plutarch and the Problematic Practice of Self-Praise (*periautologia*): The Case of Phil 3.2–21." *New Testament Studies* 60 (2014) 341–59.

Spitaler, Peter. "Welcoming a Child as a Metaphor for Welcoming God's Kingdom: A Close Reading of Mark 10:13–16." *Journal for the Study of the New Testament* 31 (2009) 423–46.

Stott, John. *Men Made New: An Exposition of Romans 5–8.* Grand Rapids: Baker, 1966.

Streete, Gail Corrington. "*Askesis* and Resistance in the Pastoral Letters." In *Asceticism and the New Testament*, edited by Leif E. Vaage and Vincent L. Wimbush, 299–316. New York: Routledge, 1999.

Taylor, Charles. *Sources of the Self: The Making of Modern Identity.* Cambridge: Harvard University Press, 1989.

Thiselton, Anthony. *First Corinthians: A Shorter Exegetical and Pastoral Commentary.* Grand Rapids: Eerdmans, 2006.

———. *The First Epistle to the Corinthians.* The New International Greek Testament Commentary. Grand Rapids: Eerdmans, 2013.

Thorsteinsson, Runar M. *Roman Christianity and Roman Stoicism.* Oxford: Oxford University Press, 2010.

Towner, Philip H. *1–2 Timothy & Titus.* IVP New Testament Commentary Series. Downers Grove, IL: IVP, 1994.

———. *The Letters to Timothy and Titus.* NICNT. Grand Rapids: Eerdmans, 2006.

Valantasis, Richard. "Competing Ascetic Subjectivities in the Letter to the Galatians." In *Asceticism and the New Testament*, edited by Leif E. Vaage and Vincent L. Wimbush, 211–29. New York: Routledge, 1999.

———. "Constructions of Power in Asceticism." *Journal of the American Academy of Religion* 63 (1995) 775–821.

Vergeer, Wim C. "The Redeemer in an 'Irredeemable Text' (1 Timothy 2:9–15)." *Neotestamentica* 50 (2016) 71–87.

Volf, Miroslav. *Exclusion and Embrace: A Theological Exploration of Identity, Otherness, and Reconciliation*. Nashville: *Abingdon*, 1996.

Weren, Wim. "Children in Matthew: A Semantic Study." *Concilium* 2 (1996) 53–63.

White, Leland J. "Grid and Group in Matthew's Community: The Righteousness/Honor Code in the Sermon on the Mount." *Semeia* 35 (1986) 61–90.

Witherington, Ben, III. *The Letters to Philemon, the Colossians, and the Ephesians: A Socio-rhetorical Commentary on the Captivity Epistles*. Grand Rapids: Eerdmans, 2007.

———. *Paul's Letter to the Philippians: A Socio-Rhetorical Commentary*. Grand Rapids: Eerdmans, 2011.

———. *A Shared Christian Life*. Nashville: Abingdon, 2012.

Wojciechowski, Michael. "Paul and Plutarch on Boasting." *Journal of Greco-Roman Christianity and Judaism* 3 (2006) 99–109.

Wolff, Christian. "Humility and Self-Denial in Jesus' Life and Message and in the Apostolic Existence of Paul." In *Paul and Jesus: Collected Essays*, edited by A. J. M. Wedderburn, 145–60. Sheffield: JSOT, 1989.

Wright, N. T. *Jesus and the Victory of God*. Minneapolis: Fortress, 1996.

———. *Paul: Fresh Perspectives*. London: SPCK, 2005.

Index